Mentoring
new
TEACHERS

Third Edition

Mentoring
new
TEACHERS

Third Edition

Hal Portner

CORWIN PRESS
A SAGE Company
Thousand Oaks, CA 91320

For information:

Corwin Press
A SAGE Company
2455 Teller Road
Thousand Oaks, California 91320
www.corwinpress.com

SAGE Ltd.
1 Oliver's Yard
55 City Road
London EC1Y 1SP
United Kingdom

SAGE Pvt. Ltd.
B 1/I 1 Mohan Cooperative
  Industrial Area
Mathura Road, New Delhi 110 044
India

SAGE Asia-Pacific Pte. Ltd.
33 Pekin Street #02-01
Far East Square
Singapore 048763

Printed in the United States of America.

Library of Congress Cataloging-in-Publication Data

Portner, Hal.
Mentoring new teachers/Hal Portner; foreword by Gerald N. Tirozzi.—3rd ed.
   p. cm.
Includes bibliographical references.
ISBN 978-1-4129-6008-3 (cloth: acid-free paper)
ISBN 978-1-4129-6009-0 (pbk.: acid-free paper)
   1. Mentoring in education—United States. 2. First year teachers—United States. 3. Teachers—In-service training—United States. I. Title.

LB1731.4.P67 2008
370.71′55—dc22   2008004902

This book is printed on acid-free paper.

08   09   10   11   12   10   9   8   7   6   5   4   3   2   1

Acquisitions Editor:	Dan Alpert
Associate Editor:	Desirée Enayati
Production Editor:	Veronica Stapleton
Copy Editor:	Lori Wingate
Typesetter:	C&M Digitals (P) Ltd.
Proofreader:	Theresa Kay
Cover Designer:	Michael Dubowe
Graphic Designer:	Scott Van Atta

Contents

Foreword

Hal Portner has a long and impressive career in the field of education. His background as a teacher, school district administrator, State Department of Education staff member, and consultant in higher education presents him as an educator eminently qualified to address the important issues underlying the preparation and induction of new teachers.

I had the pleasure of working closely with Mr. Portner in my role as Connecticut's Commissioner of Education (1983–91). He played a key role in the implementation of the state's Education Enhancement Act, passed in 1986, which dramatically raised teacher salaries as standards for the profession. In particular, he assisted in designing and implementing professional development activities and programs and the mentorship and induction model for new teachers. He also served as the coordinator of the Connecticut Institute for Teaching and Learning—which became Connecticut's major vehicle and catalyst for offering comprehensive, sustained professional development for teachers and administrators.

It is gratifying for me to see Mr. Portner utilize his expertise and hands-on involvement in writing a timely, instructive, and important book on mentoring new teachers. The book provides direction and guidance that clearly outlines how to be a mentor. The important areas of coaching, guiding, relating, and assessing are presented within a conceptual and practical framework. In effect, the author provides a workbook approach in the mentorship learning process, which draws the reader into an interactive mode. Mr. Portner's efforts are user-friendly.

The reader will be impressed with the author's practical and concrete suggestions and recommendations, his reference to a variety of techniques, and his use of learning style inventories. The various techniques described are presented in an open-ended manner, challenging the reader to further explore and expand on the myriad ideas presented.

This book will be of great service and utility to teachers who are presently serving as mentors, as well as teachers who are considering their involvement as mentors of teachers. School administrators, especially school principals, will benefit from the book as they plan induction and orientation programs for new staff, as well from its potential to engage more teachers as role models and guides for those new to the profession. Teacher-educators will find Mr. Portner's work a valuable resource or supplementary text in supervision and evaluation courses.

The induction of new teachers is arguably the most important component of a long-term comprehensive model of teacher growth and development. Regardless of the quality of the preparation of a first-year teacher, it is ultimately that initial day, week, month, and year that often predict success or failure in the classroom. Quality mentorship by experienced teachers can provide much needed support, assistance, and guidance in the formative years of teaching. To this end, Mr. Portner has made a significant contribution to the profession of teaching.

—Dr. Gerald N. Tirozzi
Executive Director
National Association of Secondary School Principals

Preface to Third Edition

Because you are reading this, I assume that you are someone who is a mentor, is going to be doing some mentoring, hasn't yet decided whether you want to be a mentor, trains and/ or otherwise supports mentors, has or would like to have a mentor (that would make you a mentee), or is just plain curious about mentoring.

Not many years ago, few educators would have fit into any of the above categories. Mentoring—if it existed at all in the culture of a school—was initiated either as an informal response to a new teacher seeking help or as assistance offered to a new teacher by an experienced colleague willing to share his or her expertise. In contrast, other professionals, like doctors and lawyers, and tradespeople, like plumbers and electricians, have been inducted into their respective fields through formal internships or by serving as apprentices "paying their dues"—both examples of programs in which novices are formally paired with mentors.

Although mentoring beginning teachers is not a new idea, over the past decade or two it has come of age—or at least experienced its adolescence. Its surge in growth has been marked with some moments of angst, but more often with emerging maturity. The evolution of mentoring can be measured not only by its maturation, but also by its proliferation.

As more and more schools and districts are establishing formal teacher induction and mentoring programs, committed leaders are seeking and drawing more and more upon proven and effective strategies and materials. I am pleased that since publication of its first edition and continuing through its second, this book, *Mentoring New Teachers,* has been among those most frequently used as a resource to support their efforts to develop strong programs.

I first became aware of the need for a new edition of *Mentoring New Teachers* when individuals and groups who read and used the book suggested that although the original material remains "right on target and extremely practical," some modifications and additions that reflect recent enhancements in mentoring knowledge and practice would make the publication even more useful. Distinguished educators who reviewed the 2003 second edition of the book at the behest of Desirée Enayati, my editor at Corwin Press, provided insightful suggestions, as did Desirée herself. This feedback was gratefully received, and together with insights from my own recent experiences in and research about mentoring, provided the focus of and material for this third edition. This upgrade contemporizes previous material and adds a substantial number of new and updated strategies, exercises, resources, and concepts. Among these additions are sections on

- The nontraditional new teacher
- Classroom observation methods and instruments
- Tools to assess learning styles
- Teacher Mentor Standards
- Mentoring's role in induction
- Confidentiality
- Mentoring student teachers
- Linking mentoring to career-long professional development

I have also updated and expanded the annotated bibliography of mentoring-related publications. Hopefully, this extensive resource will entice readers to expand their thinking about mentoring and provide practitioners with additional ways to apply the skills, behaviors, and understandings associated with effective mentoring.

WHO SHOULD READ THIS BOOK

This book is primarily for the person who already is a mentor and wants to hone his or her skills, who is going to be doing some mentoring and wants to do it well, or who hasn't yet decided whether to be a mentor and wants to know more about what mentors do.

Mentoring New Teachers is intended as a (1) self-instruction, how-to workbook for a serving or prospective mentor; (2) sourcebook for participants in and leaders of mentor training programs; (3) supplementary text for a seminar or a graduate-level course in educational leadership; and (4) practical resource for a school district's administrators, staff development coordinators, and mentoring teams. Its focus is on the mentoring behaviors associated with four critical mentoring functions: relating, assessing, coaching, and guiding. A series of exercises—supplemented by anecdotes, commentary, and examples—spans several chapters. I have designed these exercises to help the reader develop practical mentoring behaviors and construct his or her own understanding of the critical mentoring functions.

OVERVIEW OF THE CONTENTS

I have organized the elements of what it takes to be a successful mentor of new teachers into eight components: an introduction that sets the stage, four chapters that present the details of what mentors do, a fifth chapter that links mentoring to career-long professional development, a sixth chapter that suggests ways to tweak the mentoring environment, and a collection of resources that provide rich supplementary materials. After reading this book, working through its exercises, and examining its resources, you will have gained a comprehensive perspective of mentoring, a set of basic mentoring skills and tools, and a variety of practical strategies for applying mentoring's functional behaviors.

The introduction discusses what mentors do and why. It elicits from your own and others' experiences the behaviors consistent with good mentoring. Four critical mentoring functions—relating, assessing, coaching, and guiding—are introduced. The introduction emphasizes the importance of training experienced teachers to use the behaviors associated with these functions and clarifies the differences, as well as similarities, between mentoring and supervising.

Chapter 1, "Relating," stresses the important part a relationship plays in the mentoring process. Through a set of introspective exercises, you learn ways to establish trust and to pay attention to such nonverbal communication as thoughts, feelings, and body language—behaviors that help build and maintain a professionally productive relationship with a mentee. It also elaborates on the issue of confidentiality and provides insight associated with mentoring student teachers.

Chapter 2, "Assessing," provides you with a variety of ways to gather and diagnose data about a mentee's teaching, learning, and acculturation needs and preferences. The specific needs of the non-traditional new teacher are discussed. Exercises and suggestions help you determine how your mentee receives and processes information. The chapter describes how the assessing function can help you make informed mentoring decisions.

Chapter 3, "Coaching," familiarizes you with classroom observation and pre- and postobservation conferencing strategies. A series of exercises clarifies and provides the opportunity to practice behaviors that you need to help a mentee reflect on his or her performance and make decisions about his or her teaching.

Chapter 4, "Guiding," provides ways to wean a mentee from dependence on a mentor. The chapter systematically guides you through the process of directing a mentee's journey from unseasoned neophyte to self-reliant practitioner. It discusses and provides opportunities to practice diagnosing a mentee's ability and motivation levels in relation to a given situation and to use appropriate behaviors both to address the situation and move the mentee to a higher level.

Chapter 5, "Mentoring's Legacy," honors mentoring's responsibility to introduce new teachers to career-long professional development. Featured is a case study of a new teacher going through a structured process that builds his capacity to take responsibility for his own career-long professional growth.

Chapter 6, "Tips and Observations," offers a variety of actions and understandings that make mentoring more effective and more gratifying.

The resources at the end of the book include a peer-reviewed set of Teacher Mentor Standards (Resource A); an instrument for determining preferred learning styles (Resource B); the Mentor Inquiry Process—a professional development self-guide for experienced mentors (Resource C); the Connecticut Competency Instrument, which describes the teaching competencies expected of a beginning teacher that are observable in the teacher's classroom (Resource D); and an extensive annotated bibliography of mentoring-related publications (Resource E).

ACKNOWLEDGMENTS

It is with a great deal of gratitude and appreciation that I acknowledge the time, energy, and considerable expertise the following colleagues devoted to the critical review, field testing, and application of material in this manuscript. Their comments, suggestions, and insights were most appropriate and many were incorporated into the final version.

- Christine L. Brown, Assistant Superintendent of Schools, Glastonbury, Connecticut Public Schools
- William Collins, PreK–6 School Principal, Massachusetts
- Kaye Dean, Elementary School Principal, Arizona
- Randall Furash-Stewart, Middle School Teacher, Orange, MA, and The Teachers' Loft, Holyoke, MA
- Tom Ganser, Director of the Office of Field Experiences and Associate Professor in the Department of Curriculum and Instruction at University of Wisconsin–Whitewater
- Norma Gluck, Regent Emeritus, New York State Department of Education
- Judy Katzman, Adjunct, Neag School of Education, University of Connecticut
- Priscilla Miller, Director, Center for Teacher Education and Research, Westfield (MA) State College
- Robert Pauker, Educational Consultant
- Sue Teece, Induction and Mentoring Coordinator, and the entire Mentoring Team at the William E. Norris School, Southampton, MA

I especially wish to thank my wife, Mary, for her patience and support and Dr. Gerald N. Tirozzi, Executive Director, National Association of Secondary School Principals, for his advice, encouragement, and support over the years.

—Hal Portner
Northampton, MA

Corwin Press gratefully acknowledges the contributions of the following reviewers:

Kathy Grover, Assistant Superintendent
Clever R-V School District
Clever, MO

Jo Lane P. Hall, Lead Teacher
Center for Knowledge

Richland School District
Columbia, SC

Debra Pitton, Professor of Education
Gustavus Adolphus College
Saint Peter, MN

Denise Rives, Educational Consultant
Region 18 Education Service Center
Midland, TX

Erin Rivers, English Teacher
Shawnee Mission North
Overland Park, KS

Joy Rose, Retired Principal
Westerville, OH

Sharilyn C. Steadman, Assistant Professor
Florida State University
Tallahassee, FL

About the Author

 **Hal Portner** is a former K–12 teacher and administrator. He was Assistant Director of the SummerMath program for high school women and their teachers at Mount Holyoke College; and for 24 years, he was a teacher and then administrator in two Connecticut public school districts. He holds an MEd from the University of Michigan and a sixth-year Certificate of Advanced Graduate Study in education administration from the University of Connecticut. For three years, he was with the University of Massachusetts EdD Educational Leadership Program. From 1985 to 1995, he was a member of the Connecticut State Department of Education's Bureau of Certification and Professional Development, where, among other responsibilities, he served as Coordinator of the Connecticut Institute for Teaching and Learning and worked closely with school districts to develop and carry out professional development and teacher evaluation plans and programs.

Portner writes, develops materials, trains mentors, facilitates the development of new-teacher and peer-mentoring programs, and consults for school districts and other educational organizations and institutions. In addition to *Mentoring New Teachers,* he is the author of *Training Mentors Is Not Enough: Everything Else Schools and Districts Need to Do* (2001); *Being Mentored: A Guide for Protégés* (2002); and *Workshops That Really Work: The ABCs of Designing and Delivering Sensational Presentations* (2005); and editor of *Teacher Mentoring and Induction: The State of the Art and Beyond* (2005)—all published by Corwin Press.

Introduction

Have you ever had a mentor? Someone—perhaps a college professor, family member, coworker, or friend—who inspired you, helped keep you going, and showed you the ropes? In the field of education, mentors are usually veteran teachers who support colleagues new to the profession, encourage them, and help them become better teachers.

Raymond is a veteran teacher. He was selected to become a mentor for a new colleague in his school. Raymond was excited about his new role. He was also nervous because he wanted to do a good job. Raymond decided to spend a few minutes thinking about others who had helped him when he began his teaching career. He made a list of their behaviors that helped him to become a better teacher and person.

I asked Raymond to share his list with me. I was curious what the people he considered to have been his mentors did that supported, encouraged, and helped him become the fine educator he is. Raymond's list is on the next page. But wait . . . before you turn the page, take a few minutes to think about those who mentored you. What are your recollections?

What are some things a person you consider to have been your mentor did that supported, encouraged, and helped you to grow professionally? Perhaps one thing that person did was celebrate your achievements in some way. Construct your own list. Write six of your mentor's positive behaviors in the space below.

_____

_____

_____

_____

Here is what Raymond remembers about his mentors:

They made themselves available.

They listened to what he had to say.

They were encouraging and optimistic.

They seemed to know what he needed and when he needed it.

They invited him to watch them teach, then discussed with him what they did and why they did it.

They were willing to share their expertise.

They helped him set realistic goals and timelines.

They made practical suggestions.

They directed him to other people or resources when they did not have answers.

They provided him with constructive and timely feedback on his planning and teaching.

They encouraged him to take risks and to make his own decisions.

They made him think about what he was doing in such a way that it helped him consider whether there were better ways.

They helped him feel that he was not on his own. They believed in his ability to succeed.

In addition to Raymond's list, here are some attributes of good mentoring that a colleague from the private sector shared with me:

A mentor looks for signs of specialness that he can somehow work with and develop.

A mentor manages to "think out loud" in the mentee's presence.

A mentor gives honest advice when needed. A mentor does not let his [mentee] get beat up or spit out.

A mentor lets her mentee "shine." She knows the credit will reflect back on her as much as it does on the mentee.

And from an elementary school principal, these observations:

The mechanics of teaching can be taught, but the love for children cannot. Mentors who are able to communicate their caring for children are better mentors. . . . Because teaching is a new experience every time you walk into a classroom, good teachers build a repertoire of strategies and tools that they can use when they need them. Good mentors share their tools with their mentees and help them build their own repertoire.

Your list, Raymond's, and the others include a wide variety of mentoring behaviors. Successful mentors not only have an extensive repertoire of such behaviors but also use them appropriately when they interact with their mentees, when they attempt to figure out what their mentees need, when they guide their mentees' professional growth, and when they encourage their mentees to make informed decisions on their own. The protégés of successful mentors feel empowered and eventually become willing and able to identify and address their own professional problems and needs. And lo and behold, many successful mentors have discovered that when they employed behaviors that enabled their protégés to grow, their own competencies also strengthened!

SUPPORT FOR MENTORING

Between 1998 and 2004 there was close to a 25 percent increase (from 21 to 33 percent) in the number of states that mandate beginning teacher support as part of their teacher induction programs (Hall, 2005), and the number continues to grow. Although the number of states *financing* support for new teachers has not grown much over the years, there are signs that this is changing. Alabama, for example, has allocated $3.9 million in state funds to allow every first-year teacher to have a mentor during the 2007–08 school year (Act 2007-361 of the state's 2008 education appropriation bill). The Alabama mentors will be experienced teachers who will each be paid a $1,000 stipend to be a mentor to a young educator.

Both the National Education Association (NEA) and American Federation of Teachers (AFT), the nation's largest teacher unions, jointly support the establishment of programs under which all beginning teachers would be assigned a mentor. In response to state mandates and teacher union encouragement, increasing numbers of school districts have arranged for experienced teachers to help their new colleagues persist and develop beyond their difficult first year.

Idealistic considerations, state mandates, state funding, and NEA/AFT encouragement aside, much of the recent support for mentoring new teachers can be attributed primarily to two practical realities: the high rate of attrition among new teachers and the high cost of replacing them. *The New York Times* (Dillon, 2007) reports that, according to the Department of Education, "about 269,000 of the nation's 3.2 million public school teachers, or 8.4 percent, quit the field in the 2003–04 school year. Thirty percent of them retired, and 56 percent said they left to pursue another career or because they were dissatisfied" (p. 2). The large number of teachers across the country who give up on the profession every year costs the public schools an estimated $7.3 billion annually (National Commission on Teaching and America's Future, 2007). A case in point: The Clark County Nevada School System needed nearly 1,200 teachers to fill vacancies for the 2007–08 school year. And in San Francisco, the district spends an estimated $12 million to recruit, hire, and train new teachers each year to replace those who've left.

The staggering financial burden high turnover places on a district can be devastating. It diverts resources that otherwise could be devoted to books, tutors, and other instructional resources (Portner, 2005a). There are other costs, too. Constantly replacing teachers destabilizes the instructional process and places disruptive and demoralizing burdens on the system that it can ill afford. The bottom line is that it takes effective teachers to leave no child behind. And "for the students who are perpetually left behind—the ones with IEPs and the ones from under-resourced communities—they need effective teachers to stay the most" (Shyu, 2007, p. 11).

The large number of new teachers entering the profession each year will need the kind of support that *effective* mentors are prepared to provide. What is an "effective mentor" and how does a mentor become effective?

EFFECTIVE MENTORS ARE MADE, NOT BORN

In February 1997, the U.S. Department of Education's National Center for Education Statistics published its report, *Teacher Professionalization and Teacher Commitment: A Multilevel Analysis*. Among the findings of the study described in this report was that "having a mentor program to assist beginning teachers is less important for improving teacher performance and commitment than the quality of that assistance" (National Center for Education Statistics, 1997, p. viii).

So how can a school district see to it that its mentoring program is of high quality? Part of the answer is to give veteran classroom teachers the opportunity to be mentors. Experienced teachers generally take on the challenge and responsibility of mentoring with high hopes and good intentions. Classroom expertise, hope, and good intentions, however, will not by themselves guarantee effective and accomplished performance as a mentor. A dedicated, experienced teacher becomes and grows as an effective and accomplished mentor by design and training, not by chance.

Many educational leaders recognize the fallacy of assuming that veteran teachers, by virtue of years of successful experience in the classroom, automatically make good mentors for adults. Consequently, an increasing number of educational organizations at local, regional, and state levels are providing professional development opportunities for mentors. These efforts typically include distributing relevant reading materials to mentors, organizing mentoring conferences and seminars, and providing comprehensive mentoring workshops. Both the reading materials and the seminars generally aim to impart a body of knowledge germane to working with adult colleagues. This knowledge base includes such concepts as Stage Theory and Adult Development. Comprehensive workshops usually address the special knowledge of mentoring and also provide opportunities for participants to learn and develop coaching, conferencing, and classroom observation skills. Ongoing mentor training and mentor support teams arranged for by a designated mentor coordinator are especially critical to the continuous development and effectiveness of mentors and mentoring.

There is an additional aspect to mentoring that perhaps does not receive enough emphasis. This subtle and sometimes overlooked facet of mentoring has to do with understanding the purpose and function of the mentor's role in relation to that of supervisor, curriculum coordinator, and department head.

MENTORING IS NOT EVALUATING

Consider this scenario. In your district, subject coordinators are expected to serve as mentors as well as supervisors to new teachers in their departments. You are a new teacher. Aña, your mentor-supervisor, calls you into her office and gives you a list of books to use for your classes. You are disappointed with the list because, in your opinion, it does not offer the students a wide enough range of views. You and Aña have developed a good professional relationship in the short time you have been working together, and for the most part, you have found her advice and suggestions to be helpful. You would like to discuss your viewpoint about the book list, but a little twinge in the pit of your stomach reminds you that Aña soon will be filing an evaluation report on you with the principal, and you don't want to "rock the boat." You tuck the list into your pocket and walk away, trying to decide whether to accept the list and follow it closely or to substitute books of your own choosing on the sly.

A critical difference between the role of supervisor (e.g., department head, curriculum coordinator, or principal) and the role of mentor is that a mentor cannot be an evaluator. Trust and confidentiality are vital components of mentoring. No one—especially someone in a new environment trying to prove himself or herself—wants to expose insecurities and inexperience to a coworker and thus leave oneself vulnerable to possible ridicule and censure. Yet it may be necessary for a mentee to risk these behaviors in order to help the mentor understand the crux of a situation. This degree of openness may be difficult to achieve if it is the mentor's responsibility to evaluate the mentee or to recommend certification.

Here are some other distinctions between the role of mentor and evaluator.

- Mentoring is collegial; evaluating is hierarchical.
- Mentoring observations are ongoing; evaluating visits are set by policy.
- Mentoring develops self-reliance; evaluating judges performance.
- Mentoring keeps data confidential; evaluating files it and makes it available.
- Mentoring uses data to reflect; evaluating uses it to judge.
- In mentoring, value judgments are made by the teacher; in evaluation, they are made by the supervisor.

There are, of course, some commonalities between the roles of mentor and supervisor. For example, the mentor shares with his or her supervising colleagues the goal of improving the quality of the novice's teaching, often attempting to achieve that goal by helping the beginner to develop lesson plans, to select curriculum materials, and to construct assessment tools. But an effective mentor understands that although it is the ultimate goal, improving classroom performance is not enough; mentoring should also stimulate the mentee's own critical and creative thinking about how to teach and how children learn. It is the evaluation aspect of supervision that is contrary to this basic aspect of mentoring.

Some districts have instituted a program called Peer Assistance Review (PAR) that seeks to link mentoring to evaluation by adding one significant element to mentoring; mentors conduct formal evaluations and make recommendations regarding the continued employment of participating teachers. From my personal point of view, a PAR program is not mentoring, nor should it be considered mentoring—it is supervision and evaluation. In all fairness, proponents of PAR use the term *peer assistance* rather than *mentoring*, although the assisting teachers are encouraged to use mentoring behaviors.

Toledo instituted a PAR program in 1981. Several other cities, including Boston, Cincinnati, Milwaukee, Minneapolis, New York, and Rochester, have joined Toledo in instituting PAR, but as of this writing, no state has mandated it. Most of these districts provide the PAR program not only to new teachers, but also to veteran teachers who are experiencing difficulties in the classroom.

MENTORING'S ROLE IN INDUCTION

Mentoring, which commonly functions as a one-on-one relationship with a series of interactions between a new teacher and a veteran, is actually part of a larger system called *induction*. Induction includes "training for the mentor, a variety of support programs for new teachers (and their mentors) that complement and extend the mentor relationship, administrative support for the mentor program, and a district or school comprehensive plan that formulates and quantifies the expectations for the induction program" (Saphier, Freedman, & Aschheim, 2007, p. 17). A comprehensive induction program is vital to the successful retention and development of new teachers. By its very nature, induction requires the involvement of a variety of people in a variety of roles.

This book, *Mentoring New Teachers,* is not about induction, per se. Rather, it concentrates exclusively and extensively on the specific functions and responsibilities of the most complex and intricate role in the induction process: mentoring.

There are several excellent publications for those wishing to delve into the intricacies of induction, including the following:

New Teacher Induction: How to Train, Support, and Retain New Teachers (Breaux & Wong, 2003)
Supporting Beginning Teachers: How Administrators, Teachers, and Policy-makers Can Help New Teachers Succeed (Brewster & Railsback, 2001)
Training Mentors Is Not Enough: Everything Else Schools and Districts Need To Do (Portner, 2001)
Beyond Mentoring: Comprehensive Induction Programs: How to Attract, Support, and Retain New Teachers (2nd ed., Saphier, Freedman, & Aschheim, 2007)
Leading the Teacher Induction and Mentoring Program (2nd ed., Sweeny, 2007)

Descriptions of these and other publications having to do with teacher induction can be found in Resource E: Annotated Bibliography.

THE MENTOR'S PRIMARY ROLE

It is simplistic to think of a mentor as a guru, a master teacher, at whose feet one sits and to whom one poses occasional questions, hoping to absorb the mysteries of the art. The role of mentor as "expert-who-has-the-answers" has its place and value, but a new teacher needs to develop the capacity and confidence to make his or her own informed decisions, enrich his or her own knowledge, and sharpen his or her own abilities regarding teaching and learning. Purposefully bringing a mentee to this level of professionalism is the mentor's primary role.

A mentor functions best in this role by relating, assessing, coaching, and guiding. These four functions draw upon the eclectic body of knowledge that informs the mentoring process and are carried out through a variety of skills and behaviors.

WHAT MENTORS DO: THE FOUR MENTORING FUNCTIONS

Relating

Mentors build and maintain relationships with their mentees based on mutual trust, respect, and professionalism. Relating behaviors create an environment that allows mentors to develop a genuine understanding of their mentees' ideas and needs and encourages mentees to honestly share and reflect upon their experiences.

Assessing

Mentors gather and diagnose data about their mentees' ways of teaching and learning; they determine their mentees' competency and confidence to handle a given situation; they identify unique aspects of the school and community; and they take note of the school district's formal and informal culture, procedures, and practices. Assessing behaviors ensure that the mentees' professional needs and learning styles are identified so that mentoring decisions can be based on a thoughtful consideration of a variety of data.

Coaching

Mentors help their mentees fine-tune their professional skills, enhance their grasp of subject matter, locate and acquire resources, and expand their repertoire of teaching modalities. Coaching behaviors allow mentors to serve as role models to their mentees; to share relevant experiences, examples, and strategies; and especially to open new avenues by which mentees can, through reflection and practice, take responsibility for improving their own teaching. Mentors wean their mentees away from dependence by coaching them through the process of reflecting on decisions and actions for themselves and encouraging them to construct their own informed teaching and learning approaches. Teaching involves constant decision making. The mentor places the responsibility for decision making with the mentee. Decisions about teaching are driven by reflection. The coaching skill of the mentor is to ask the right questions the right way, and at the right time—questions that encourage the mentee to reflect on his or her decisions.

Guiding

Guiding behaviors acknowledge and act on the mentee's degrees of ability and willingness to perform. Guiding behaviors stimulate the mentees' creative and critical thinking, empower them to envision future situations, encourage them to take informed risks, and help them build the capacity to develop perceptive decisions and take appropriate actions.

These mentoring functions do not occur in isolation. They consistently overlap and complement each other during the mentoring process.

TEACHER MENTOR STANDARDS

In the spring and summer of 2002, Jean Casey and Ann Claunch, coordinators of the resident teacher program at the University of New Mexico, and I held a series of discussions around the impact of mentoring on teaching and learning. The inquiry was grounded by the conviction that effective mentoring improves the decision making abilities and behaviors of the mentee, which in turn results in enhanced performance and achievement by the mentee's students. Our discussions and research centered on identifying the attributes of a mentor that contribute to effective mentoring. We agreed that these attributes include not only the observable behaviors of a mentor, but also behaviors that are generally unobservable, such as a mentor's decision-making process.

Our inquiry culminated in the formulation of a set of Teacher Mentor Standards based on the core propositions developed by the National Board for Professional Teaching Standards (1989). It was our belief that these standards would establish a foundation for mentoring new teachers that (1) extends mentoring beyond emotional support, encouragement, and help with routines; (2) provides guidance for best practice in teacher-mentoring programs; and (3) challenges mentors to continue to develop their own mentoring abilities.

In order to confirm that the Standards were built on a *real-world* foundation, we set aside a period for peer review. The process began with a thorough analysis and editing by Barry Sweeny, director emeritus of the International Mentoring Association. The Standards were then reviewed and validated by a number of other researchers, consultants, and practitioners including professors of education in Florida and Utah, assistant district superintendents of schools in Illinois and Connecticut, a cochair of a statewide teacher induction committee, coordinators of student teacher field experiences in Oklahoma and Wisconsin, a staff development coordinator in a South Dakota school district, a nationally acclaimed mentor trainer and consultant, and a school mentoring team leader in Massachusetts. The resultant Teacher Mentor Standards can be found in Resource A.

Standards, functions, and behaviors notwithstanding, ultimately a successful mentor must possess an additional attribute—one that is fundamental to mentoring's primary purpose. When all is said and done, a mentor, upon reflecting on his or her mentoring experience, must see himself or herself as having been not only a master teacher who may have had some answers, but also one who acted on the belief that learning takes place best between and among colleagues exploring together. This book is written in that spirit.

CHAPTER ONE

Relating

Rasheed had always wanted to teach, and now he had landed his first teaching job. In spite of his excellent student teaching experience, he found himself overwhelmed by the activities and responsibilities of the first few weeks. The formal orientation to the school and bus tour of the town helped a little, but for the most part, he felt that he was operating in the classroom without sufficient information and with little support.

He had been assigned Tanya as a "mentor." Tanya was an experienced teacher who, Rasheed was told, would help him through the first few months. Rasheed met Tanya briefly during orientation. "Don't worry, you'll do just fine," she told him. "We'll set up a schedule of meetings to discuss how I can be of help to you. Meanwhile, don't hesitate to come see me any time you have any questions."

Even though Rasheed did have questions and occasionally experienced feelings of insecurity, he was reluctant to burden his mentor with his problems. When they had their first meeting, Rasheed glossed over the difficulties he was having with class management—after all, he did not want to appear incompetent. Tanya was aware of his problems with classroom discipline, but not wanting to give the impression that she was a "prying know-it-all," she too avoided the topic. Consequently, although Rasheed and Tanya met regularly and exchanged pleasantries, they never did have a meaningful discussion about his classroom management concerns or, for that matter, about any other issue. It was no surprise, then, that the first few months of teaching were somewhat chaotic for Rasheed.

Mentoring requires interaction. But in order to be productive, mentor-mentee interactions must take place within a relationship that includes mutual trust, honesty, respect, and a joyful willingness to work together. It is important to build and maintain a productive mentor-mentee relationship because it provides the mechanism for—and is the source of energy behind—a mentor's ability to carry out the other mentoring functions.

Unless a solid working relationship is established from the start, the mentoring process runs the risk of being like that experienced by Rasheed and Tanya: perfunctory and routine. Even if a relationship is initially well established, it needs to be maintained. Otherwise, over time, interactions between mentor and mentee will tend to deteriorate into workaday obligations. Therefore, your first, and potentially most challenging, responsibility as a mentor is to develop and maintain a productive relationship with your mentee.

So how do you go about developing and maintaining a productive mentoring relationship—one that you and your mentee will cherish as an opportunity for collegial interchange and professional growth? In this chapter, we will explore four powerful sets of behaviors—establishing trust, paying attention to thoughts and feelings, honoring confidentiality, and communicating nonverbally—that can help you build a beneficial collegial relationship with your mentee.

ESTABLISHING TRUST

Before we consider how to build trust in a mentor-mentee relationship—and why trust is an important part of that relationship—we need to be clear as to what constitutes trust. What does trust mean to you? What is it like to be in a relationship where trust exists? In what ways do you relate differently to a person you trust from the way you relate to someone you do not particularly trust? The following exercise will help answer these questions.

Exercise 1.1   How You Act When You Trust

Think about someone you know and trust. Keep that person in mind as you complete the following sentence:

Because I trust (the person you have in mind), I . . . (List several behaviors, feelings, thoughts, and expectations you experience because you trust that person.)

_____

_____

_____

_____

_____

_____

_____

_____

_____

_____

_____

_____

_____

_____

Note: I've done this exercise, too, but don't peek at my list on the next page until you have created your own in the space above. There are no "right" answers, of course, because we all have our own perception of trust. I am sharing my list just to provide another viewpoint.

Here is my list:

Because I trust Mary, I . . .

freely share my experiences and my aspirations.

tend to use humor more often.

listen to and respect her opinions, even though I may disagree.

will ask for and appreciate her opinion and advice.

will lend or give her a cherished possession.

try to understand her meanings and intent by probing for more information.

am willing to offer more information if asked.

feel at ease with her.

feel comfortable asking her for help.

Now that you and I have more or less defined trust in terms of its associated behaviors, the next question we need to answer in keeping with our focus on building a productive mentor-mentee relationship is how to get your mentee to trust you.

Exercise 1.2   Behaviors That Elicit Trust

Complete the following sentence:

When I want someone to trust me, I . . . (List several behaviors you exhibit when you want someone to trust you.)

_____

_____

_____

_____

_____

_____

_____

_____

_____

_____

_____

_____

_____

_____

_____

_____

Note: Yes, I have developed a list for this exercise also. It is on the following page. Wait, don't turn the page yet. Complete your list first.

Here is my list:

When I want someone to trust me, I . . .

walk the talk; that is, I do what I said I would do. As a friend of mine puts it, "trust is the residue of promises kept."

respect confidentiality.

respond to the other person's statements and questions to their satisfaction before introducing another topic.

express my feelings as well as my thoughts.

recognize and respect his or her feelings and ideas, even though I may not agree with them.

Now, between your lists and mine, we have a litany of trust-building behaviors.

Why is trust so important an ingredient in a relationship? It is important because it allows both the mentor and mentee to recognize, accept, discuss, and consequently work to improve ineffective practices. After all, it takes trust to ask for help, to expose your insecurities and inexperience to a coworker, and to leave yourself vulnerable and open to ridicule. It may well be necessary for your mentee to risk these behaviors in order to help you understand the crux of a situation.

PAYING ATTENTION TO THOUGHTS AND FEELINGS

Do you remember what was going through your mind and the emotions you experienced that first day on the job as a teacher? Too many years ago? Well, then, how about a more recent situation—like when you first thought about being a mentor. The following exercise may help you recall that occasion.

Exercise 1.3   Relive the Experience

When the possibility of being a mentor first occurred to you, do you remember what it felt like? What were some of your concerns, thoughts, and feelings?

Read the following scenarios. As you read, try to recall some of the thoughts and feelings you had when you first considered being a mentor. Jot down your reflections in the space provided on page 18.

Scene 1: Gloria, a high school biology teacher, picks up the memo she found in her school mail box this morning. It reads:

MEMO TO: Gloria

FROM: Building Principal

RE: Invitation to mentor a new teacher

Several new teachers will be joining our staff when the school year begins next fall. As you know, the district has recently instituted a Beginning Teacher Support Program that matches newly hired teachers with experienced ones. I feel you would make an excellent mentor for one of our new colleagues. Please come to my office during your scheduled free period next Tuesday when we can discuss details.

Gloria opens her scheduling book and enters a note about meeting with the principal on the following Tuesday.

Scene 2: Next Tuesday, Gloria's free period. She rereads the memo, tucks it into her scheduling book, tucks the scheduling book under her arm, and heads toward the principal's office.

"Me, a mentor?" she thinks to herself as she walks down the hall.

"Hey, why not! The principal thinks I can do it. After all, good mentoring is probably very much like good teaching. Here is my chance to help a new teacher by passing on what I've learned over the past 10 years."

(Continued)

(Continued)

"I am looking forward to being an 'official' mentor. I've helped beginning teachers before, but I've never really had the formal responsibility. But what if I do a poor job? How will I feel about myself? What will others think of me?"

"Hey, why am I worrying? I'm good at what I do. I know how to teach; I have good rapport with my students and colleagues."

"I remember back when I first started teaching. I had doubts about whether I would ever become a competent teacher, let alone survive my first year in the classroom. I really felt that I was on my own. I did make it finally, but I sure wish I had someone there for me, someone I felt comfortable with. I guess a mentor is someone that I could call on when I needed help, information, or just reassurance."

"I know I should be more confident. I've heard and read enough about mentoring new teachers to understand what's involved. So why do I feel so apprehensive?"

"There are so many questions I have. When I meet with the principal, I'm sure some of these questions will be answered, but will the new teacher—my mentee—and I get along? I probably will get to watch my mentee teach, but how would I feel about having him or her watch me teach? There must be some expertise a mentor needs beyond good interpersonal skills and experience as a teacher. What are they? Do I have them? If not, will I have the opportunity to acquire them?"

Gloria reaches the principal's office and enters with a mixture of anticipation and trepidation.

_____

_____

_____

_____

_____

Did any of Gloria's reactions to taking on that new role resonate with ones you experienced at the time? If you are a veteran teacher like Gloria, you probably experienced both anticipation and trepidation when faced with a new and important professional challenge. Imagine, then, what it must be like for a new teacher today. In addition to the many complex issues you probably faced when you became an educator, today's first-year teacher—your mentee—will be working from day one with an increasingly diverse student population and probably facing the challenge of integrating students with special needs into his or her classroom.

Your mentee will have questions about such issues as curriculum, materials, parent meetings, school policy, and the community. Your mentee will also have thoughts and feelings about many other aspects of his or her new profession. He or she will probably ask the questions, but unless you two have developed a relationship with a history of attending to relevant thoughts and feelings, the discussion runs the risk of producing only superficial information from your mentee, thus allowing you only limited insight into the gist of the question. In other words, thoughts and feelings add depth to communication.

A powerful way to build and maintain a productive mentoring relationship is to share thoughts and feelings about teaching. It is important that you really listen to what your mentee tells you—not just to the words, but also to the feelings.

For example, responding to the following statement from your mentee: "I will be teaching exactly what I had hoped for—sixth-grade math and science," with: "It sounds as though you're excited about meeting your students and getting started," will show the mentee that he or she is being heard at a deeper level than just the content of the words. Once those feelings have been addressed and accepted, the way may well be open for the mentee to voluntarily provide additional information and express some concerns that he or she was not comfortable doing before. So, not only is this attention to feelings helpful to the development of a good relationship, it also is an excellent way to draw out the mentee's specific needs and concerns.

Of course, you could just come right out and ask the new teacher what needs or concerns he or she has about teaching math and science to sixth graders, and you may get some useful information. But until the mentee trusts that feelings will be heard and honored, it may be difficult for him or her to risk exposing any insecurities to a stranger. Indeed, such a direct question—no matter how well intended—may even provoke additional feelings of insecurity.

By way of illustration, suppose that Sharon is Rolf's mentor. Sharon sits next to Rolf in the teachers' room one morning before school, nods a good morning to her mentee, and asks, "How are your classes going? You're working on writing, aren't you?"

"Oh, the students are writing OK," Rolf replies, "but I wish they would pay more attention to spelling."

"Don't worry about that," says Sharon. "Their spelling will improve in time. Can I get you a cup of coffee?"

Rolf sighs, "No, thanks. I had some earlier."

Sharon did not do a very good job of mentoring here, did she? Let's back up and consider what she could have said to acknowledge feelings, build trust, and encourage Rolf to consider a wider range of options.

When Rolf said, "The students are writing OK, but I wish they would pay more attention to spelling," Sharon should have let Rolf know that she was aware of the feelings beneath the words by saying, for example, "It sounds as though you are concerned about your students' poor spelling. Go on, tell me more."

As their conversation progressed, Sharon should have periodically checked out her understanding of what Rolf was saying by restating in her own words what she had heard (e.g., "If I hear you correctly, you are saying that . . ." "Let's see if I understand you. Are you saying . . . ?" "When you said . . . , it seemed you were implying . . ."). Sharon then would have allowed Rolf to correct, clarify, or validate his restatement.

Suppose Rolf asks, "Do you think I should assign the students extra homework in spelling?"

Sometimes it is effective to answer a question with another question. This encourages your mentee to probe for his own answer. The questions you ask should be open-ended in that they require more than a "yes," "no," or other one-word answer. Starting your question with "why" or "how" will serve this purpose. How do you think Sharon could respond to Rolf's question about assigning extra spelling homework? Write your thoughts in the space below.

Here are some other relating behaviors that Sharon, the mentor, would find productive:

- Use descriptive rather than evaluative or judgmental state-ments. For example, if she is giving feedback to Rolf about how he disciplined a disruptive student, Sharon might begin by saying, "I noticed that you took a big breath just before going over to talk to (the disruptive student)."
- When Rolf says or indicates something to her, Sharon needs to be aware that her mentee expects her response to be rele-vant to what he just said. By not honoring that expectation, Sharon risks cutting off further discussion of that topic, inhibiting further discussion in general, and eroding a little of the relationship.
- Occasionally, Sharon should check out the accuracy of any assumptions she may have about her mentee's unspoken thoughts or feelings. She can do this by paraphrasing back to her mentee what it is she assumes and allowing him to con-firm or clarify.
- Above all, Sharon must—as all mentors must—respect confidentiality.

CONFIDENTIALITY

Confidentiality is such an important element of the mentor/mentee relationship, and so prone to misunderstanding, that its meaning and subtleties cannot be taken for granted. One of the first conversations a mentor and mentee have should lead to mutual agreement as to how each views and intends to exercise confidentiality. Here is a suggested set of issues for a discussion between mentor and mentee about ground rules for confidentiality:

- How much of what we discuss should remain only between us? For how long?
- Under what circumstances would it be OK for either of us to talk with a colleague (e.g., principal, another mentor, another teacher) about our mentoring relationship?
- What will the mentor do if asked by an administrator to pro-vide an evaluation of the mentee?

- Under what circumstances and to what extent would it be acceptable for either of us to share information with a supervisor or administrator about the other's performance or behaviors? For example, in the event the mentor determines that a student or another person is in physical, emotional, or psychological danger because of a mentee's action or inaction, it is the mentor's obligation to bring the situation to the attention of the proper individual. Should the situation be reported without informing the mentee?

A district mentoring team might find it helpful to develop its own confidentiality ground rules such as the following example.

In general, mentors will not discuss the new teacher's performance with anyone, including school and district administration, except under the following conditions (Ribas, 2006):

1. A mentor will be able to discuss, in confidence and **with the new teacher's knowledge**, any aspect of the teacher's performance with other members of the mentoring team. (Note: In this case, the mentoring team will not include an administrator or supervisor.)

2. A mentor, **with the new teacher's knowledge and permission**, may discuss the new teacher's performance with resource professionals whose job it is to help teachers.

3. A mentor, **with the new teacher's knowledge**, may discuss the new teacher's performance with appropriate administrators if, in the mentor's professional judgment, the academic growth and development, social well-being, or physical safety of the students or other members of the school community are at risk.

THE STUDENT TEACHER DILEMMA

In just about every teacher preparation program in the United States, schools of education require and arrange for their students, typically in their senior year, to *student teach* in a public or private school preservice program. This field-based experience is usually a credit-course and is graded. The major responsibility for day-to-day guidance of student teachers rests with the classroom teacher, usually referred to as a *cooperating* teacher. In addition to assisting the student teacher, the cooperating teacher is also expected to report on the student teacher's performance and recommend a grade. From what I have been able to ascertain, not many states require training for cooperating teachers. One exception is Section 1–10–145d-8-x of The Regulations of Connecticut State Agencies, which defines student teaching as "supervised full day practice teaching, *with a trained cooperating teacher*, as part of an [approved] educator preparation program" (emphasis mine). Connecticut's cooperating teachers are also encouraged to participate in the state's mentor training program. In some other states, the unofficial criteria are that cooperating teachers have a minimum number of years of experience and be willing to take on a student teacher. To exacerbate the situation, not all higher education institutions offer training for cooperating teachers that includes coaching or mentoring.

The role of a cooperating teacher includes responsibilities similar to those of a teacher-mentor, that is, to develop and provide a teaching/learning atmosphere that supports dialogue and discussion, promotes the sharing of advice and constructive feedback, and encourages open communication. There is one important difference, however, between mentoring a first- or second-year teacher and mentoring a student teacher. The mentor of a student teacher is involved in evaluating and grading; the mentor of a new teacher is not. The student-teacher/cooperating-teacher relationship is impacted by the need to share information about performance with others who will use that information to evaluate the student teacher; therefore, the relationship cannot be entirely confidential. Nevertheless, it must be based on openness and trust in order to work to its best advantage.

Cooperating teachers need to make it clear to their charges that their role is to help them succeed. The cooperating teacher's dilemma, of course, is twofold: (a) gaining and keeping a student teacher's trust while giving up some aspects of confidentiality and (b) not letting the need for a trusting relationship interfere with evaluation and grading responsibilities. This is why training of cooperating teachers is so important and must include methods of establishing openness and trust within the student-teacher/ cooperating-teacher relationship.

An effective way to encourage trust and openness is to regularly check to determine whether student teachers feel they are receiving the help they need. Five factors for mentoring practices identified by Hudson, Skamp, and Brooks (2005) provide a handy checklist for this purpose. The factors—Personal Attributes, System Requirements, Pedagogical Knowledge, Modeling, and Feedback—and their attributes are listed below. Does your student teacher perceive that you

(Personal Attributes)

- are supportive
- are comfortable in talking
- are attentive
- instill confidence
- instill positive attitudes
- assist in reflecting

(System Requirements)

- discuss aims
- outline curriculum
- discuss policies

(Pedagogical Knowledge)

- guide preparation
- assist with timetabling
- assist with classroom management
- assist with teaching strategies
- assist in planning
- discuss implementation
- discuss content knowledge
- provide viewpoints
- discuss questioning techniques
- discuss assessment
- discuss problem solving

(Modeling)

- model rapport with students
- display enthusiasm
- model a well-designed lesson
- model effective teaching

- model classroom management
- demonstrate hands-on approaches
- use syllabus language

(Feedback)

- observe teaching for feedback
- provide oral feedback
- review lesson plans
- provide evaluation on teaching
- provide written feedback
- articulate expectations

COMMUNICATING NONVERBALLY

Suppose you run into someone you haven't seen in a while and the person smiles and says to you, "So tell me, how are you, and what have you been up to lately?" Before you can answer, the smile disappears; the person glances at his or her watch, and then starts looking around, but not at you. Which message do you trust? What feelings are being expressed? I don't know about you, but to me the nonverbal message would come across much more strongly than the spoken words.

There is power in body language. When gestures and words conflict, confusion enters the relationship; when they are in harmony, trust is communicated and received. Notice your mentee's facial expressions and general posture while he or she is speaking to you. Is he or she relaxed? Tense? Distracted? Even when a person's demeanor seems to be in sync with their words, the way he or she sits or moves can add other dimensions to what is being said at the time.

You may want to check out the accuracy of how you perceive your mentee's nonverbal expressions. Doing so will give your mentee the opportunity to clarify and perhaps to expand upon his or her comments. Keep in mind, however, that in and of itself, a specific body movement or expression does not necessarily indicate a specific meaning. Nonverbal cues should be considered together with other gestures and in context with spoken words. In addition, there are regional and cultural variations in the use and meaning of gestures and expressions that need to be considered. In general, however, most people will take someone leaning toward them while they are talking as meaning *I am hearing you and interested in what you are saying.* Crossed arms, by contrast, may connote discomfort with—or rejection of—an idea.

To what extent are you aware of the reactions your use of body language evokes in others? For example, when you are listening to your mentee and nod your head occasionally, chances are he or she feels that you are really paying attention to his or her words. The following exercise will show you the power of body language.

Exercise 1.4   The Power of Body Language

When you find yourself in the kinds of situations described below, try using the body language I suggest and see what happens. In each of the two scenarios, notice that you consciously change or shift from one position to another. Take note of any changes in the content and quality of conversation that occurs after you shift. If your mentee is the other person in this exercise, be sure to explain, after it is over, what you were doing and why. You share this information with your mentee in order to reinforce trust and to dispel any misunderstanding that may have occurred. It would be advantageous to have the exercises videotaped, if doing so would not interfere with the activity, because it would be helpful to review the interactions from the viewpoint of an uninvolved observer.

Situation A: During a conversation, the other person begins telling you about something that happened earlier. Lean slightly toward the speaker. Look at him or her with interest. Occasionally, nod your head.

In the middle of one of the speaker's sentences, shift. Lean back, look away, and cross your arms. If the speaker asks you whether anything is wrong (or words to that effect) answer, "Oh, no. Please continue," but keep your body language aloof.

Situation B: During a conversation, you notice that the other person is sitting rather stiffly with fingers clasped together or grasping the arms of the chair. His or her feet are planted squarely on the floor, and he or she appears somewhat uncomfortable. Mirror the other's manner; assume the same posture and demeanor.

Early into the conversation, begin to gradually shift your body. First, unclasp your fingers. Wait for a corresponding relaxation of hands by the other person, then cross one leg over the other toward the person. Continue gradually moving your body into a more relaxed position, making slight changes each time your colleague mirrors your last adjustment.

When you carry out this exercise, you will probably notice that your body language communicated strong messages and elicited definite responses. In conversations with your mentee, if your words are honest, your body language will automatically reinforce what you say and contribute to the development of trust in your relationship.

Unless proven otherwise, trust that your mentee will be honest with you, will follow through with what he or she has agreed to do, and will honor the commitment made to the mentoring process. Your behaviors must engender the same level of trust in your mentee.

A CHECKLIST OF RELATING BEHAVIORS

✓ To the best of your ability, do you do what you say you will do?

✓ If you find that you cannot follow through on a promise, do you let your mentee know and suggest an alternative?

✓ Unless given permission by your mentee, do you treat in confidence anything of a personal or professional nature that he or she tells you or you observe? (Of course, you will need to use your judgment in the event the situation involves a matter of safety, endangerment, or professional malpractice.)

✓ When your mentee offers some information or opinion or asks a question, do you respond to his or her statement or query before going on to another topic?

✓ Where you feel comfortable doing so, do you express your feelings as well as thoughts about a topic under discussion?

✓ Do you acknowledge and respect your mentee's feelings and ideas, even though you may not agree with them?

✓ Do you probe for thoughts and feelings as well as facts when discussing professional issues?

✓ When your mentee offers some important information, do you encourage your mentee to say more in more detail?

✓ Do you periodically check out your assumptions about what your mentee was thinking and feeling as well as what was said? (You can do this by restating in your own words what you heard and assumed and then allowing your mentee to correct, clarify, or validate your restatement.)

✓ Do you respect your mentee's ability to make decisions by encouraging him or her to probe for his or her own answers?

✓ Do you use descriptive rather than evaluative or judgmental statements when reviewing a mentee's decision or behavior?

✓ Do you let your body language reinforce the intent of your words?

✓ Are you sensitive to mixed messages—contradictory words and gestures—both from yourself and from your mentee? (You can avoid sending conflicting messages by being honest in what you say.)

✓ If you think you perceive disharmony between words and body movement, do you check out your assumptions and give your mentee the opportunity to clarify?

A MENTORING RELATIONSHIP IS A SERVING RELATIONSHIP

Rachel Naomi Remen, clinical professor of family and community medicine at the University of California, San Francisco, in a talk given at the "Open Heart, Open Mind" conference in San Diego, California, in July 1995, made an observation about the caregiving relationship that applies equally to the mentoring relationship. She said, "Serving is different from helping. Helping is based on inequality; it is not a relationship between equals . . . . Helping incurs debt. When you help someone they owe you one. But serving, like healing, is mutual. There is no debt. I am as served as the person I am serving. When I help I have a feeling of satisfaction. When I serve I have a feeling of gratitude. These are very different things." Remen went on to say, "Serving is also different from fixing. When I fix a person, I perceive them as broken. There is distance between ourselves and whatever or whomever we are fixing [and] we cannot serve at a distance."

CHAPTER TWO

Assessing

I f you were to ask a group of beginning teachers what kind of help they need from a mentor, many would tell you—as they consistently tell me and other researchers—that they need help with discipline, classroom management, and lesson planning. In addition, most would indicate that they need information about school policies and procedures, that they appreciate timely feedback, and that they hunger for friendly support.

Does this mean that all new teachers have the same needs and therefore can be treated the same? Of course not. "Treating individuals individually is exactly what mentoring is all about. It is the best form of support for professional growth because it is customized to address the strengths and needs of *each* learner" (Sweeny, 2007, p. 10). You function as an assessor when you gather and analyze data in order to find out what it is that *your* mentee knows or doesn't know and can or can't do. You function as an assessor when you identify resources and strategies that will support *your* mentee's assessed needs. And you function as an assessor when you determine how *your* mentee will best take in, process, and communicate information.

THE NONTRADITIONAL NEW TEACHER

Traditionally, beginning teachers enter the profession directly from college. "One day, they [are] blue-jeaned students groaning about professors' lectures and anticipating weekend parties. [The next], they are teachers who are expected to look, behave, and speak as professionals" (Brock & Grady, 2007).

More and more, however, beginning teachers are apt to be older, more mature, have had other occupations, or have raised families before entering the teaching profession. Maria always loved working with kids. The 37-year-old was working as a youth minister at a church when she saw a newspaper clipping about a shortage of classroom teachers in her midwestern city. Maria enrolled in an alternative teacher preparation program offered in collaboration between the city's public schools and the regional state college. David, age 50, left his job as a securities investment representative to take part in the same program as Maria.

Maria and David had college degrees and careers prior to enrolling in the alternate route to teaching program. Others in the program had taught at the university level, had been classroom aides in area schools, or had led training for federal agencies or private sector companies.

Others who have chosen teaching as a second career are retirees from the corporate sector, some with encouragement from their companies. For example, IBM's Transition to Teaching program, established in 2005, offers up to $15,000 in subsidies and other corporate support for departing employees who want to take up teaching. Robert had worked for IBM for 32 years and designed interactive marketing programs for the company's Web site. He holds degrees in both electrical engineering and computer science. He recently retired, took advantage of IBM's program, and is now teaching math to middle and high school students in Westchester County in New York.

Emily was a teacher's aide in an inner city elementary school. She had taken college courses in the past, but did not complete the requirements for a degree. Emily was encouraged by the school's principal to go back to school, get her degree, and become a teacher. She did, and now teaches in that principal's school.

Given their advantages of age and experience, most of these alternate route teachers will adjust rather readily to their new working environment. Alternate route programs, however, are typically of short duration. Transition into full-time teaching, often without the benefit of student-teaching opportunities, happens quickly. Attention to an older beginning teacher's pedagogical needs is especially important.

There are experienced teachers who may have transferred to your school from your own or another district or even from another state. Because they are mature and experienced, they are likely to be relatively competent as teachers, but they are still new as far as the school's students, culture, policies, and procedures are concerned.

They require mentoring appropriate to their needs, and each individual will have different needs.

Other nontraditional teachers who join your faculty may be former teachers who have decided to return to the profession after several years away, perhaps at home raising children. Because they have taught before and are older, it is tempting to treat them as seasoned veterans. Actually, unless they have kept current, they will find that much has changed in the profession during their absence from teaching. Despite their maturity, assessment of these reentry teachers may well align them with beginners, and they should be mentored accordingly (Brock & Grady, 2007).

GENERIC NEEDS OF NEW TEACHERS

In spite of differences in individuals and degrees of experience, there are categories of needs that many new teachers have in common. The following exercise will introduce you to some of these. Your mentee will most likely share in a number of them.

Exercise 2.1   Stuff That Makes Novices Nervous

Below are eight categories that typically contribute to the angst of being a new teacher. I have indicated a situation and an example of a specific need that relates to each category, a need that you can reasonably anticipate your mentee will have. Your task is to add an additional example for each category (you do not need to suggest a solution, although you may, if you wish).

Category: Curriculum (the specific content to be taught in a course in the mentee's school)
  Situation: The mentee teaches sixth-grade science to a class of students from diverse backgrounds with a variety of developmental abilities.
  Example of need: How to select lesson content that is suitable for the diverse levels of students' cognitive development and appropriate to their various social, emotional, and physical development.
  Your situation:
  Your example of need:

(Continued)

(Continued)

Category: Instruction (the strategies and methods by which the curriculum is taught)

Situation: Some of your mentee's students learn primarily from visual stimulation, others from auditory stimulation. Most move from one to another with forays into a kinesthetic style.

Example of need: How to teach in ways that will engage the entire range of student learning styles in the class.

Your situation:

Your example of need:

Category: Lesson Planning (mapping out the activities, sequence, use of resources, instructional strategies, and student assessment aspects of a lesson)

Situation: Students in this middle-school mathematics class come into the classroom immediately after lunch. They are usually lethargic and slow to get into the lesson.

Example of need: How to begin a lesson so that students will focus on its content with anticipation.

Your situation:

Your example of need:

Category: Student Assessment (determining the extent to which students understand and can apply the lesson's content)

Situation: Your mentee teaches geography. The students are doing well in her class and they enjoy the subject. She is aware, however, that the students do poorly in the language arts (which she does not teach).

Example of need: How much attention should be paid to spelling and grammar when grading a geography test?

Your situation:

Your example of need:

Category: Classroom Management (making sure that the classroom provides a safe and orderly place in which to learn)

Situation: Your mentee spends an inordinate amount of time distributing and collecting papers and taking care of other classroom routines.

Example of need: How to physically arrange the classroom in order to improve its functionality.
Your situation:
Your example of need:

Category: School Policy (the routines and procedures school personnel are expected to follow)
Situation: Your mentee has arranged a field trip for her students but is uncomfortable about the legal aspects involved.
Example of need: What is involved, and who is responsible for arranging transportation and insurance for a field trip?
Your situation:
Your example of need:

Category: Parents and Community (the nature and degree of involvement, responsibility, and authority parents and community have vis-à-vis the school system)
Situation: Your mentee would like the opportunity to meet his students' parents and guardians.
Example of need: How to get more parents to attend the annual "open house."
Your situation:
Your example of need:

Category: Emotions (the stresses, feelings, and attitudes experienced while carrying out various aspects of the profession)
Situation: Your mentee is scheduled for his first formal evaluation by the principal. He is really nervous and has asked for your guidance.
Example of need: How to prepare for, cope with, and recover from an evaluation by one's supervisor.
Your situation:
Your example of need:

SPECIFIC NEEDS OF YOUR MENTEE

In the above exercise, we listed several examples of categorical concerns that we can assume are shared by many new teachers. But what additional concerns does *your* mentee have?

One way to find out what your mentee needs is to ask him or her. Another way is to keep your eyes and ears open for clues. For example, if you want data about teacher-student interaction, you can go into the classroom and observe these dynamics for yourself. Another source—perhaps the best source of all—from which to get a realistic sense of classroom dynamics is the students themselves.

If you and your mentee are willing to solicit and respect honest student feedback, a process called Small Group Instructional Diagnosis, or SGID, affords the opportunity to gain some insights about classroom dynamics not otherwise obtainable. SGID was pioneered in the 1970s at the University of Washington by Joseph Clark. It was conceived as a midcourse adjustment strategy and has become a regular feature of hundreds of institutions of higher education throughout the country.

For the following exercise, I have modified the SGID process to make it applicable to middle and high schools. If your mentee is a prekindergarten, kindergarten, or elementary teacher, I encourage you to experiment with my adaptation and modify SGID even further so that it will resonate more readily with the developmental stage of those younger students.

Exercise 2.2   Get the Students' Perspective

On a prearranged day about halfway through the school year, during the last 30 minutes of the class and in the absence of the first-year teacher, form students into groups of four to six. You can use cooperative learning groups if they already exist in the class. The reason for using small groups is that they place the extremes of student opinion within the context of group consensus. The procedure also increases validity.

Have each small student group select a recorder, then discuss these three questions: (1) What helps you learn in this class? (2) What gets in the way of your learning? and (3) What can be done to help you learn better? Following 10 minutes of discussion, ask each group to come to consensus on its answers.

Before beginning, make it clear to the students that (a) the discussion will focus on what goes on in the classroom, not on the teacher, and (b) it will be up to the teacher to decide what, if anything, he or she will do about the students' responses.

When all groups have completed their discussions (or when the designated time has expired), have the recorders report their groups' answers to the entire class. Write the comments on the board as they are presented. When all the groups have presented their comments, summarize and clarify until all agree on a class response to each question.

While you are working with the students in the classroom, have your mentee, working alone, ponder the following: (1) What will the students say it is that helps them learn in the class, and what do I (the mentee) think will help? (2) What will the students say it is that gets in the way of their learning, and what do I (the mentee) think it is? (3) What will the students suggest doing that will improve their ability to learn, and what do I (the mentee) suggest?

The class's small-group discussion is preceded by a pre-SGID conversation and followed by a post-SGID discussion, both of which take place privately between you and your mentee. The pre-SGID meeting provides an opportunity to talk about the purpose of the process and to discuss goals, class activities, and any sensitive aspects or conditions that might apply. The meeting also offers an opportunity to change the generic questions to ones that relate to specific aspects of the class and to agree on how the information obtained will be treated.

The post-SGID meeting consists of a discussion of the information gathered. The intent is to understand the students' perspectives, to reflect on any differences between student and instructor perceptions, and to decide whether to make any changes based on the activity. The conversation should include a discussion about strategies for any anticipated change and consider what the teacher might say when talking to the students about the SGID's results during the first 5–10 minutes of the next class.

It is important to understand that SGID is not a student evaluation of the teacher. It is a voluntary, confidential assessment process for the mentor-mentee's use only. The information generated by a SGID can be ignored or considered together with other data as an indicator of needs. At the very least, SGID can generate thoughts about possible changes in teaching strategies and/or potential adjustments in a classroom's learning environment. It also offers students a good example of group decision making and consensus building.

GATHERING RESOURCES

Another aspect of the assessing function is to identify and have readily available the information and materials that will help your mentee address his or her needs as they arise. The following exercise will help you identify and gather material and information that you will want to have available when your mentee asks for or needs them.

Exercise 2.3   A Treasure Hunt for Resources

Take another look at the categories in Exercise 2.1. This time, we will use these categories as a checklist for a treasure hunt. The idea is to create a file of information that will be useful to your mentee.

Keeping this purpose in mind, search throughout your school, district, and community for resources that will help address each category of need. Also, check out the Internet for additional material. If you do not know where to start looking on the Web, try http://www.ed.gov (U.S. Department of Education), http://www.nea.org (National Education Association), or http://www.aft.org (American Federation of Teachers). These sites provide links to a wealth of educational materials. If you don't already know how to find more Internet sites, ask your local computer guru to tell you about search engines. If you do not personally have access to the Internet or your school cannot provide you with access, try your local public library.

Then, in the numbered spaces provided, write the names of one or two resources that exist for each category. Last but not least, get the resources and file them away for your mentee.

Category: Curriculum
Example of resource: The results of students' most recent standardized and criterion reference tests.
Another example: Copies of the National Curriculum Standards for the mentee's subject area, your state's curriculum

framework and standards, and your local district's pertinent curriculum guide(s).

1. _____

2. _____

Category: Instruction
  Example of resource: The name of a teacher or teachers in your district who recently completed a series of workshops on instructional strategies and is willing to share that information.

1. _____

2. _____

Category: Lesson Planning
  Example of resource: Instructions on how to access the regularly updated files of lesson plans available on various Internet sites.

1. _____

2. _____

Category: Classroom Management
  Example of resource: Suggestions on how to rearrange classroom furniture and equipment to facilitate interactive learning.

1. _____

2. _____

Category: School Policy
  Example of resource: Emergency procedures in case of accident or illness involving students with physical disabilities.

1. _____

2. _____

(Continued)

(Continued)

Category: Parents and Community
  Example of resource: Recent history, policies, and activities of the local Business and School Partnership Program.

  1. _____

  2. _____

Category: Emotions
  Example of resource: Information regarding the stress management program and other psychological counseling services available at no cost to city employees.

  1. _____

  2. _____

In addition to the items you identified in Exercise 2.3 above, there are some resources that would be helpful to a new teacher if only they were available. An example of one such potentially valuable resource that is usually nonexistent or hard to find is a tangible collection of insights about the culture and atmosphere of the new teacher's school and community. If your school has a booklet, a CD/video, or an annotated scrapbook that portrays the school's unique personality and special qualities, by all means procure and file a copy. If not—or even if it does—the next exercise will prepare you to introduce your mentee to the special qualities of his or her new working environment.

Exercise 2.4   This Is Us

Write a short description of the mentee's school and community in terms of their special characteristics and qualities, rather than demographics and statistics. Include maps, photographs, and sketches. Complete the following sentences to focus your thoughts.

1. The students in this school . . .

2. Their parents . . .

3. The teachers in this school . . .

4. The nonteaching professional staff, secretaries, and custodians . . .

5. The school's major claim to fame is . . .

6. The first thing that would inspire a stranger upon entering the school is . . .

7. Teaching in this school is like . . .

8. The surrounding community is . . .

9. Some interesting places in town are . . .

10. Local community support for education comes from . . . in the form of . . .

Among several books written especially for the beginning teacher are *The First Days of School* by Harry and Rosemary Wong (1999) and *Being Mentored: A Guide for Protégés* by Hal Portner (2002). Others titles can be found in Resource E: Annotated Bibliography.

YOUR MENTEE'S LEARNING PREFERENCES

Adults—and children, too, for that matter—have distinct preferences for the way they take in, interact with, and respond to stimuli in a learning environment.

For example, suppose you want to help your mentee learn to develop a lesson plan. Would he or she prefer concrete examples or benefit more from theories and abstractions? Would starting with the *big picture* be more helpful than supplying step-by-step instructions? Would your mentee rather talk about the process or read about it? If you are aware of your mentee's particular learning preferences, you can communicate with him or her more directly by using materials, words, and phrases that will resonate at a deeper level of understanding.

One way to find out how your mentee prefers to approach a specific learning situation is to ask. Assuming you and your mentee have an honest and trust-based working relationship, this is an excellent assessment strategy. For example, you could reply to a request for help planning lessons by saying, "You wanted to talk about developing lesson plans. Do you want to discuss lesson plans in general? Would you like me to critique one of yours? Would you prefer me to show you how I do it, or do you have some other thoughts or specific questions?"

Another way to determine learning preferences is to inquire whether your mentee has recently completed one of the instruments that have been developed to identify personality and learning styles and if so, whether he or she would be willing to share its results with you. Four of the most often administered instruments of this type are

> *The Dunn, Dunn, and Price Learning Style Inventory* (adult version) investigates an individual's learning style as influenced by environmental, emotional, sociological, physical, and psychological elements.

> *Kolb's Learning Style Inventory* organizes responses into two bipolar concepts—concrete experience versus reflective observation and abstract conceptualism versus active experimentation. An analysis of responses classifies learners as accommodators, convergers, assimilators, or divergers.

> *Gregorc's ORGANON* describes the way one perceives images cognitively from concrete to abstract and suggests that information is ordered either in a sequential fashion or in a random way.

> *The Myers-Briggs Type Indicator* organizes an individual's personality preferences into four bipolar concepts: extroversion versus introversion, sensing versus intuition, thinking versus feeling, and judgment versus perception. The results are often used to predict behavior and attitudes.

Although it is generally agreed that one can apply different learning modes in various situations and individuals can change their preferred learning style over time, familiarity with both your mentee's and your own preferred learning styles can suggest how to frame questions and comments and when to propose developmentally paced activities. Knowing your own preferred style is especially important if your mentee's is different from yours, in which case you can adjust your input more easily.

MODES OF COMMUNICATION

Suppose your mentee, Frank, says to you, "The kids have been giving me a tough time. I'm planning to rearrange the seating in my classroom: girls on one side and boys on the other." You want to encourage Frank to think about the ramifications of his plan. Which of the following statements would best communicate this to Frank?

   1. "I see what you're saying, Frank. But look, will this result in the type of classroom situation you envision?"

   2. "I hear what you're saying, Frank. But tell me: Will this result in the type of classroom situation it sounds like you want?"

   3. "I'm in touch with your concern, Frank. But help me get a handle on what it is you expect; will this result in the type of classroom situation you hope for?"

The answer is: It depends on Frank's sensory mode at the time.

Pictures, Words, and Feelings

Our memory banks consist of pictures, words, and feelings. When we communicate with others, both as senders and receivers, we go into these memory banks to search for the pictures, words, or feelings that contain appropriate information. Then we take in or put out that information through our senses—primarily visual, auditory, and feelings (tactile and emotional). We normally do not remain in the same sensory mode throughout an interaction. In fact, most of us develop a particular sequence of sensory modes through which we process various experiences.

When I speak to another person, the words I use usually include sensory predicates such as *see*, *hear*, *feel*, *look*, and *listen*. If my words are congruent with the particular sensory mode of the listener at the time, I can speed up the whole communication process. The listener does not have to translate my information into his or her sensory mode in order to understand.

A learning style instrument I have found particularly useful in this regard can be found in Resource B. It is the Learning Style Inventory, developed in 1995 by Richard Oliver for the Student Learning Assistance Center, San Antonio College, San Antonio, Texas. This instrument measures and categorizes the ways people take in and process information into visual, auditory, and tactile preferences.

Another, more subtle way to assess learning modes is called *Neuro-Linguistic Programming* (NLP). NLP is a behavioral model that, among other things, suggests that by observing eye movements, a person can quickly determine which of the three modes—visual, auditory, or feeling—another person is using to input, process, and output information. NLP was foreshadowed by Richard Bandler and John Grindler (1975) who studied the use and effect of language and nonverbal communication by successful therapists. The concept was further developed in cooperation with Robert Dilts, Leslie C. Bandler, and Judith DeLozier and published in 1980 under the title *Neuro-Linguistic Programming.*

You probably have noticed that during conversations, people will periodically break eye contact and shift their eyes momentarily to another position. NLP postulates that peoples' eyes move off center while accessing some bit of information and that the direction to which an individual shifts his or her eyes corresponds to the sensory mode being accessed. Dilts, Bandler, and DeLozier (1980) contend that generally speaking, when a person's eyes have shifted up and to their right or left, they are accessing internal visual imagery. When a person's eyes move laterally to their right or left, or down to their left, they are accessing internal auditory modes. And when a person is accessing feelings, their eyes will shift down and to their right. For you visually oriented learners, Figure 2.1 may present a clearer picture.

Although I do not advocate using NLP as a foolproof assessment technique, I do feel comfortable recommending that you learn more about it and consider its use in conjunction with other assessment strategies. At the very least, familiarity with NLP can help you understand that your mentee accesses various sensory modes while processing information and that the way you phrase a statement can communicate more effectively if it resonates with the mode in play at the time.

Figure 2.1   Eye Movements and Sensory Modes

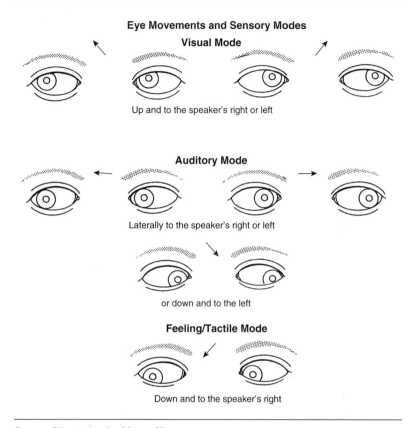

Eye Movements and Sensory Modes

Visual Mode

Up and to the speaker's right or left

Auditory Mode

Laterally to the speaker's right or left

or down and to the left

Feeling/Tactile Mode

Down and to the speaker's right

Source: Illustration by Nancy Haver.

SUMMARY

You are assessing whenever you take steps to anticipate what your mentee needs in order to grow professionally. Assessing behaviors include these:

- Taking into consideration the probability that your mentee will experience many of the concerns common to most beginning teachers—concerns such as those that fall within the categories of curriculum, instruction, lesson planning, classroom management, school policy, interacting with parents and community, and emotions

- Employing a variety of methods to identify your mentee's specific needs—methods such as asking direct questions, observing classroom and other professional performance, and eliciting student perceptions
- Acquiring and developing a variety of resources from a variety of sources to share with your mentee—resources such as those that will help him or her clarify content, determine instructional strategies and activities, acquire and use instructional resources, manage student assessment and classroom environment, understand and follow school policy, work with parents and community, and handle the stresses, feelings, and attitudes experienced while carrying out various aspects of the profession
- Determining your mentee's specific learning preferences—preferences such as those diagnosed by reliable and validated personality and learning style instruments, elicited by directly asking the mentee, and observed by paying attention to shifts in sensory mode and other body language clues

It is also important to assess not only what kind of mentoring your mentee needs, but also when he or she needs it. Chapter 4, "Guiding," examines this aspect of the assessing function in detail.

CHAPTER THREE

Coaching

Coaching: where the rubber meets the road; where it all comes together, baby; where . . . well, you get the idea (feel free to add your own favorite cliché). The point is, coaching is the mentoring function where your relating, assessing, and facilitating behaviors are applied directly to improving your mentee's performance.

COACHING ASSUMPTIONS

- Coaching places responsibility for decision making with the mentee.
- Coaching, like teaching, involves constant decision making driven by the feedback loop of action, result, adjustment.
- A major coaching skill is to ask the questions that will guide mentees to uncover their expectations, beliefs, and perceptions thereby empowering them to make their own informed decisions.
- Change resulting from reflection is not remediation.

Your goal as a coach is to develop your mentee into a self-reliant teacher. By *self-reliant teacher*, I mean a teacher who is willing and able to (a) generate and choose purposefully from among viable alternatives, (b) act upon those choices, (c) monitor and reflect upon the consequences of applying those choices, and (d) modify and adjust in order to enhance student learning.

The athletic coach develops the equivalent of self-reliance in his or her charges by using every opportunity to *raise the bar*; that is, when the athlete can perform at a particular level of ability, the coach sets a higher standard and challenges the athlete to meet it. The mentor of new teachers also coaches by raising the bar.

THE COACHING CYCLE

As a mentor-coach, your function is to observe your mentee perform and help him or her reach higher standards. Observing and raising the bar on your mentee's performance include not only noting and improving classroom behaviors, but also looking at and fine-tuning the reflection, problem-solving, and decisionmaking processes that take place before and after that class. This process—Preobservation Conference, Classroom Observation, and Postobservation Conference—is often referred to as *the coaching cycle*.

THE PREOBSERVATION CONFERENCE

Because you and your mentee will have established and maintained a trusting relationship, it is likely that an opportunity will arise for you to observe one of your mentee's classes. Within a few days prior to the scheduled classroom observation, you and your mentee should meet privately for about 20 to 30 minutes to discuss the upcoming event. Your objective here is to get your mentee to express and clarify learning objectives, fine-tune teaching strategies, anticipate student behaviors, firm up plans for monitoring student learning, and consider ways to adjust instruction.

During this preobservation conversation, your function as a mentor-coach is to ask probing questions in ways that will not only encourage your mentee to come up with ideas to enrich the lesson plan, but will also provide him or her with the opportunity to gain confidence as a reflective practitioner who thinks through the consequences of his or her plans and actions and makes modifications based on thoughtful consideration of outcomes. The following example will illustrate this process.

Suppose that you are going to observe Frank, your mentee, teach his high school American history class. You schedule a preobservation conference for the day before your classroom visit. At the start of the conference, you state your objectives—to clarify learning objectives, fine-tune teaching strategies, anticipate student behaviors, firm up plans for monitoring student learning, and consider ways to adjust instruction—and ask Frank whether he has any particular concerns about your being in his classroom the next day. You also ask him if there is anything in particular he would like you to pay attention to during your time in the classroom.

Once these issues are addressed, you ask Frank this open-ended question (i.e., a question phrased in a way that elicits information, thoughts, and/or feelings, and cannot be answered with merely a "yes" or "no"): "What do you expect your students to know and be able to do by the end of the class tomorrow?"

Your reason for asking this question is not only to find out what to expect when you observe the class, but also to provide your mentee with an opportunity to determine for himself whether he is clear about desired student outcomes.

Frank replies, "This lesson is on the ratification of the U.S. Constitution. I expect students to know when the Constitution was ratified and to know why the Federalists were concerned about what the results of the ratification vote would be and what they did to try to sway the vote their way."

Not bad. You could go into Frank's class with an idea of what his learning objectives are. But you are not just a data gatherer here; you are a mentor in coaching mode! What you want now is to get Frank to expand his concept of the lesson's big picture while, at the same time, have him clarify in his own mind exactly what he wants the students to learn, what he will do to facilitate student learning, what materials he will use, what he expects students to do to demonstrate what they have learned, and how he might modify his teaching accordingly. So you ask Frank more questions—you raise the bar.

Here are some suggestions to help you ask bar-raising questions in ways that will achieve your objective:

1. Pick up on a critical word or phrase from your mentee's reply to your previous question and probe for more detail or clarity. For example, Frank mentioned the Federalists and their concern. Your follow-up question can lead Frank to clarify the extent to which he has considered continuity from one lesson to the next, for example, "What have the students learned so far about the Federalists?" The critical word or phrase may also suggest a question that probes for the extent

to which Frank has planned a specific teaching strategy, such as "How will you get across to the students the reasons for the Federalists' concern?"

2. Press for specificity. Ask, for example, "What do you want to happen when you . . . ?" "What if it happens this way instead?" "What is the sequence of events that will take place within the lesson?" "How would you feel if . . . ?" "What has led up to and will follow this lesson?" "What student behaviors do you hope to see or hear?" "How will you know what students have learned and whether they can apply that learning?"

3. Be patient. After asking your question, wait for the answer. There is power in silence; this is when reflection happens.

4. Acknowledge and validate answers by restating them in your own words. Try recognizing feelings in the same way.

5. Avoid using judgmental phrases such as, "Wouldn't it be better to . . ." or "I can't believe you expect that strategy to work." Instead, allow the mentee to be his or her own judge by using phrases such as, "When you carry out this activity, what sort of student involvement do you hope for?"

6. Resist the temptation to offer advice (there are exceptions, of course. See the section, "When to Show and Tell," later in this chapter).

7. Summarize and acknowledge ideas, feelings, and decisions before ending the meeting.

The following exercise provides an opportunity to practice some of these important conferencing skills.

Exercise 3.1   Ask Clarifying Questions

Sarah, your mentee, is a music teacher. During the conference with Sarah prior to observing her sixth-grade music class, you say, "Sarah, tell me about your plans for this lesson."

Sarah replies, "I want the students to listen to Mozart and appreciate his music."

You want Sarah to clarify her objectives, so you ask, "After the lesson is over, what will the students know and be able to do that they couldn't before?"

Sarah thinks for a moment and replies, "My learning objectives are to have students recognize a piece of music as Mozart's and be able to explain how they can tell."

Continuing on with the above conversation, construct a probing, open-ended question relating to each of the lesson components below that will likely cause Sarah to reflect and respond with some specificity:

Instructional activities

Information about materials and how they will be used

Expected student behaviors

Plans to assess student learning

Alternative instructional possibilities

THE INITIAL CLASSROOM VISIT

In his study of teacher concerns, Fuller (1969) found that during their first couple of months, most new teachers experience such *survival* concerns as *How am I doing?* and *Will others approve of my performance?* Imagine, then, how your mentee probably feels the first time you are in her classroom to observe. It should come as no surprise that no matter how well the relationship is progressing or how smoothly the preobservation conference went, chances are that, on one level, your presence will be perceived as judgmental—possibly even threatening. These feelings can be compounded when your mentee knows that you are there to observe her professional behavior. Here is how you can ease your mentee's initial concerns.

- Make your first foray into the classroom short and agenda-free. Make it a *visit* rather that an observation. Be clear that its *only* purpose (and be honest about this) is to acclimate both students and teacher to your presence. Stay no longer than ten or fifteen minutes; take no notes; conduct no pre- or postobservation conferences. Be there as a *nonentity*, not as an analyzer or teacher-helper. Resist answering such questions as *How did I do?* or *Do you approve of my performance?* either during or after your visit. Instead, remind your mentee about the purpose of your being there.

- Don't impose yourself. Make this visit by invitation only. Tell your mentee what you would like to do and why. Let her know that you will be *officially* observing her class at a later date but that before you do, you would like her and her students to be at ease when you are present. Ask that if she prefers, she can invite you in for another such visit before you schedule an initial formal observation.

- Invite your mentee to visit *your* class, following the same ground rules as when you were the visitor. Later on, after you have conducted a couple of formal observations, you can invite your mentee to actually observe your class and have the opportunity to process with you what she has observed.

FOCUSED CLASSROOM OBSERVATIONS: WHEN AND HOW

"Doing effective practices at the wrong time is not effective" (Sweeny, 2005, p. 132). The first three or four months of the school year is too soon for formally observing a new teacher's classroom. This time is more effectively used for developing mutual trust, building a solid professional relationship, and addressing security and logistical issues and procedures. "Typically, after the first couple of months when the policies of the school and the routine of the classroom are more or less familiar, new teachers are more focused on concerns related to curriculum, instruction, and assessment" (Dunne & Villani, 2007, p. 44). January or February is soon enough for that first scheduled observation.

Mentoring is a multiyear process. The coaching cycle (preobservation conference, observation, postobservation conference) should continue on for at least a second and possibly a third year, so don't be in a hurry to conduct that first classroom observation.

Focused Observations

When you observe, you do so to collect data. The first few times you observe, however, don't overwhelm your mentee by collecting and feeding back every little detail. Eventually, it may be useful to compose a verbatim transcript of what was said and done, when it was said and done, and by whom (a technique called *scripting*), but initially, it is much more effective to focus on one specific area of concern that has been agreed upon during the preobservation conference. For example, data collection might center on such classroom dynamics as an individual student's involvement in the lesson, curriculum or instructional decisions, or specific aspects of the teacher's lesson plan.

Data Collection

There are various publications that contain instruments and techniques that you can use to help collect data during an observation. Among these are *Another Set of Eyes* (Costa, Garmston, Zimmerman, & D'Arcangelo, 1988) and Correia and McHenry's (2002) *The Mentor's Handbook*.

Of course, you can construct your own data collection instruments. For example, if you want to collect data on verbal interactions and classroom activities, use a seating chart and a set of straightforward symbols to diagram the sequence and flow of questions, answers, and other conversations.

To illustrate: Larry, a 43-year-old retired U.S. Army officer, is just beginning his second career as a ninth-grade Algebra I teacher. His students—and even a couple of teachers—refer to him as "Captain Larry" behind his back—but never to his face. Figure 3.1 is the instrument Larry's mentor developed to collect data during one of her observations.

Figure 3.1   Data Collection Instrument: Classroom Interaction

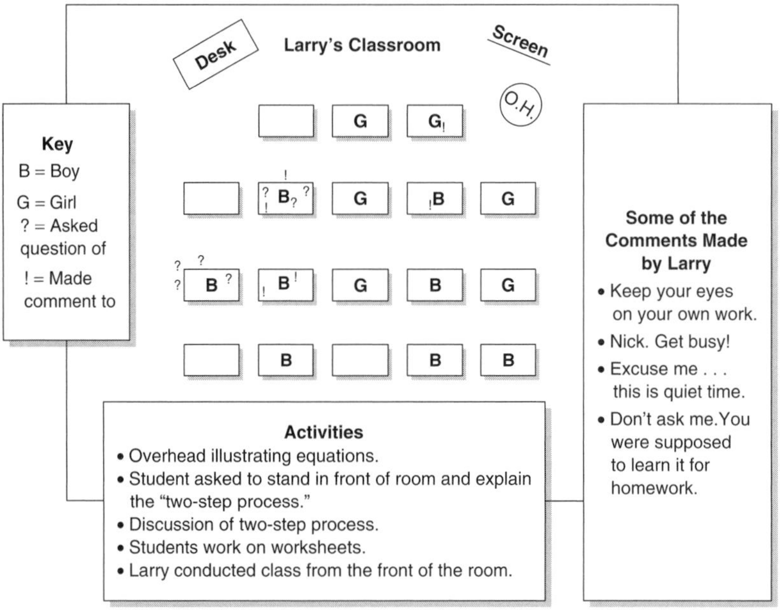

Suppose you want to collect data during an observation about the nature of what the teacher says to students and when. Kara, a first-year teacher, was concerned about these aspects of her comments to students in class. Together, Kara and her mentor, Kim, developed a checklist (Fig. 3.2) to help focus on the concern. Kim used the instrument to collect data on Kara's verbal behavior during class. At two-minute intervals, Kim checked the category that most closely described Kara's comments at the time and noted any pertinent circumstances related to a comment. Two-minute intervals between checks gave Kim an opportunity to note the circumstances around each instance. Kim gave a copy of the completed instrument to Kara and during their postobservation conference, Kim facilitated Kara's reflection on the data.

Another way to gather data during an observation is to write a focused narrative description of what transpires during the class that relates to a particular concern. For example, Luis, a first-year teacher, expressed concern during a preobservation conference as to whether he was providing effective routines and transitions and whether students were observing the classroom norms he had established. Here is the mentor's narrative focusing on an observation of

Figure 3.2   Data Collection Instrument: Verbal Behavior

						Listening	
	Giving	Giving	Answering			to	
Time	Information	Directions	Questions	Praising	Disciplining	Student	Notes
8:45							
8:47							
8:49							
8:51							
8:53							
8:55							
(etc.)							

Verbal Behavior

Teacher_____

Class _____ Date _____

routines, transitions, and norms in Luis' eighth-grade science class. The narrative was shared with Luis and served as the nucleus of their postobservation conference.

Date: February 4   *Class Period: 3rd*

The bell rang signaling the start of the period and the class immediately came to order. Luis reviewed yesterday's homework assignment (the formation and classification of rocks) then asked that "a volunteer" from each group select a rock from among those on a shelf and bring it back to their table. There was some confusion. Luis modified his instruction: "The person whose first name is last alphabetically, get the rock." After some minor confusion and good natured comparing of names, the rocks were selected. One boy, Paulo, tossed his rock loudly on the table. It slid and fell off.

Luis distributed a form to each student and instructed them to "pass your rock around the table and, without any discussion, decide what classification it falls under. Then on the form, (1) write your name, (2) check the box next to the rock's classification, (3) list the rock's characteristics that puts it in that class, and (4) write a brief description of the geological conditions that probably formed the rock." Several students looked confused. Some raised their hands, but were not called on. Two students asked for permission to sharpen their pencils. Luis allowed them to do so, one at a time.

Luis walked around the room, stopping for a moment at each table, then said: "Okay. Pencils down. Now share your answers with others at your table, talk it over, and come to agreement on the correct answer."

After allowing time to complete their task, a member of each group reported their table's consensus to the class.

Five minutes before the end of class, Luis started collecting the forms. Several of them had been crumpled or torn. When asked why, one student answered: "Mine had the wrong answers. Besides, you didn't say you were going to collect them."

Luis assigned homework for the next day. The bell rang. Luis instructed the students to return the rocks to the shelf on the way out.

Video-recording is yet another way to gather data. Video-recorded observations can provide some advantages over traditional real-time observations. For example, classroom observations don't allow observers to back up and review what they've seen. That means that postobservation discussions are only as good as your memory and your notes. A video is a visual record of what actually went on.

Video recordings can also enable your mentee to focus on the lesson from the student's point of view. Ellen Moir (2007), executive director of the New Teacher Center at the University of California at Santa Cruz, provides an example of such an instance. She was asked by a mentor how to help a mentee whose "major problem is her personality and her voice, which is very annoying and monotonous." "To help her," Ellen replied, "you need to gather evidence of her practice, which the two of you can study together. One way to do this is to videotape a lesson. Some teachers are uncomfortable watching themselves, but you might persuade her (gently) that we need to see how we appear to our students, and videotaping is a powerful way to do that."

Note: When planning to video-record a classroom, obtain signed permission to video-record their children from the parents or guardians of the students.

SOME OBSERVATION CONSIDERATIONS

While in your mentee's classroom, you are an objective observer— a human video camera—recording what is going on. Your mentee should be advised ahead of time if you intend to take written notes. Because of the preobservation conference, you have a good sense of how the lesson is expected to proceed, so seat yourself in a position to best observe its unfolding.

Be aware that your presence in the classroom, however unobtrusive, will have some influence on what is being observed. When you observe a class, you actually observe a class being observed.

Resist the temptation to become a participant. It is difficult to participate and observe objectively at the same time. Also seductive—and potentially disruptive—is the inclination to envision what you would do if you were teaching the class.

What do you look for in addition to something your mentee may have asked you to observe? If you focus on defects or weaknesses, you are observing your mentee in terms of what is wrong with him or her. Then you find yourself behaving like a pathologist, trying to diagnose symptoms and causes and hypothesizing remedies. What you really need to be interested in is the extent to which quality learning takes place. Therefore, what you look for first is evidence of student learning, then consider what is contributing to or obstructing the process. Filter all this through the information you derived from the preobservation meeting. Now you are ready for the postobservation conference.

THE POSTOBSERVATION CONFERENCE

Your classroom visit has taken place. Prior to observing your mentee in action with students, you met with your mentee to clarify learning objectives, teaching activities, use of materials, expected student behaviors, and plans for monitoring student learning and adjusting instruction. Now, as soon after the observed lesson as possible, you meet again to debrief the event and continue the important coaching function.

Your goal here is to encourage your mentee to assess the effectiveness of the lesson, to identify factors that contributed to and interfered with student learning, and to consider why he or she may have used alternative instructional strategies at times. Any feedback you give will be in the form of what you saw or heard. Stick to objective facts. Keep your opinions of what went on during the class to yourself. Avoid telling your mentee what you think should have been done.

Your methodology during the postobservation conference, as it was during the preobservation conference, is to probe with open-ended questions. Here is an example of a series of questions designed to raise the bar:

How do you think the lesson went?

Why do you think it went the way it did?

How do you know that was the reason?

When you . . . , the students reacted by . . . . Why do you think that happened?

What did you expect would happen when . . . ?

Were there any surprises?

Help me understand what you took into account when planning this particular activity.

I noticed that you altered your prepared lesson plan during (activity X).

If you could teach this lesson again, what, if anything, would you do differently?

Why?

What conclusions can you draw from the way the lesson went?

What conclusions can you draw from our meeting today?

When asking a question to elicit reflection, you need to be careful not to ask in a way that puts down or belittles your mentee. For example, asking your mentee, "If you teach this lesson again, don't you think requiring more activity on the part of the students will help them learn better?" implies that he or she didn't plan as well as you would have; or the students didn't learn very well so he or she must be a poor teacher; or how could the mentee have overlooked something this obvious? Asking a question embedded with such implied negative overtones speaks more to the emotions than to reason and creates resistance and resentment—hardly an atmosphere conducive to productive reflection. A better way to phrase such a question is, "If you teach this lesson again, will you do anything differently?" or "When you planned this activity, what expectations did you have for student involvement?" Then you can follow up with, "Do you see any correlation between student involvement in the lesson and the extent of student learning?" The following exercise will help you avoid the use of negative overtones in your questions.

Exercise 3.2   Avoiding Embedded Negatives

Rephrase the following questions to remove any negative overtones:

Can't you come up with a better way to do that?

_____

_____

Why didn't you see that you miscalculated when you planned to have students exchange seats?

_____

_____

That probably won't work. Do you have any idea of what you might do instead?

_____

_____

WHEN TO SHOW AND TELL

There will be times when your wisest role as a mentor-coach will be that of *expert*, the experienced master teacher who chooses to pass on your considerable expertise to the novice by showing or telling what to do and how to do it. For example, you *show* how it should be done when your mentee observes you teaching a class. You *tell* what you are going to do when you brief your mentee prior to the class. And then you reflect aloud on what you did during a meeting with your mentee after teaching the class. In this example, you show and tell as well as model the behaviors of a self-reliant teacher.

Here is another example of a situation that would benefit from your direct advice. Your mentee is scheduled for a formal evaluation two days from now and has a specific weakness that is certain to be judged adversely if not corrected. Your best strategy here is to alert your mentee to the situation, tell him or her how to correct the weakness, and provide whatever support you can, including emotional support.

If your mentee tells you flat out (perhaps in a pleading voice or even verging on panic) that he or she really wants you to *show and tell* how to handle a particular situation, do it. For example, suppose your mentee has been unsuccessful in his or her attempts to correct an undesirable classroom situation, is in despair, and seeks your advice.

The following exercise provides an opportunity to practice generating some advice you can give your mentee under such circumstances. The exercise is based on material from the Connecticut Competency Instrument (CCI), the set of indicators and defining attributes developed by the Connecticut State Department of Education for the assessment of beginning teachers. Sections from the CCI are reprinted, with permission from the Connecticut State Department of Education, as Resource D.

Exercise 3.3   Sharing Your Expertise

Listed below are several indicators of competencies that are observable in a beginning teacher's classroom performance. After each indicator, I give an example of an unsuccessful application of that indicator. Based on your own experience and knowledge as well as my suggestions above, record after each example what you would tell the mentee to do in order to improve that situation. To start things off, I have supplied what I would say in the first situation.

Indicator: The teacher communicates clearly, using precise language and acceptable oral expressions.

Example of unsuccessful application: When giving directions, the teacher often communicates with vague and ambiguous statements that leave students unsure about what they are being asked to do.

This is what I would tell the mentee to do: "Next time you give directions, do these three things: First, make a point of stating the directions in a sequence of steps, that is, 'First do this'—wait until it is done or questions clarified—'then this'—wait until it is done or questions clarified. Second, tell the students precisely what outcome you expect. For example, 'When you finish—and you will finish before the end of this class—you will hand in your paper with the answers to all 10 questions legibly written and clearly numbered 1 through 10.' Finally, ask a student to restate your directions in his or her own words. Clarify the student's restatement if necessary."

Now you complete the other items in this exercise.

Indicator: The teacher establishes and maintains positive teacher-student and student-student interactions.

Example of unsuccessful application: Students direct sarcastic and disparaging remarks toward one another.

What you would tell the mentee to do:

_____

_____

_____

_____

_____

_____

Indicator: The teacher establishes and maintains appropriate standards of behavior.

Example of unsuccessful application: The teacher responds to similar behaviors in different ways. Students seem uncertain as to what consequences to expect.

What you would tell the mentee to do:

_____

_____

_____

_____

_____

_____

Indicator: The teacher keeps students engaged in the activities of the lesson.

Example of unsuccessful application: Students who finish an activity early are left to their own devices until the other students are finished.

What you would tell the mentee to do:

_____

_____

(Continued)

(Continued)

_____

_____

_____

_____

Indicator: The teacher effectively manages routines and transitions.

Example of unsuccessful application: Ten to fifteen percent of class time is usually spent passing out and collecting materials.

What you would tell the mentee to do:

_____

_____

_____

_____

_____

_____

Indicator: The teacher presents appropriate lesson content.

Example of unsuccessful application: Student responses and behavior indicate that the teacher uses vocabulary and concepts well above the level of students' cognitive development.

What you would tell the mentee to do:

_____

_____

_____

_____

_____

_____

Indicator: The teacher provides a structure for learning.

Example of unsuccessful application: Students seem confused regarding the purpose of the lesson content.

What you would tell the mentee to do:

_____

_____

_____

_____

_____

_____

Indicator: The teacher develops the lesson to promote achievement of the lesson's objectives.

Example of unsuccessful application: Although students usually enjoy the activities of a lesson, test results indicate they are not achieving the lesson's objectives.

What you would tell the mentee to do:

_____

_____

_____

_____

_____

_____

Indicator: The teacher uses appropriate questioning strategies.

Example of unsuccessful application: Much of the time, the teacher answers her own questions before the students have time to respond.

(Continued)

(Continued)

What you would tell the mentee to do:

_____

_____

_____

_____

_____

_____

Indicator: The teacher monitors student understanding of the lesson and adjusts instruction when necessary.

Example of unsuccessful application: The teacher recognizes that students are not understanding the lesson, but continues on with the lesson as planned.

What you would tell the mentee to do:

_____

_____

_____

_____

_____

_____

COACHING ADULTS

Because you are a mentor or are contemplating becoming one, I can assume that you like a challenge. So how about a little test? True or false: Adults and children have the same orientation to learning.

The answer is false. Adults carry with them a different time perspective and set of experiences from that of children, which in turn produces a difference in the way adults approach learning. An important implication here is that just because someone is a good teacher of children, that doesn't automatically make them a good coach of adults.

The following exercise—a continuation of our little true-false test—will acquaint you with some general characteristics of adult learners. A mentor who understands how an adult takes in and processes information can better coach his or her mentee in ways that communicate directly and clearly.

Exercise 3.4   How Adults Learn

Here are some assumptions about adult learning characteristics. Indicate in each blank whether that statement is true or false.

_____1. Adults would rather learn something in order to solve a particular problem than learn something just for the sake of learning.

_____2. Adults will take longer to learn something new than will children.

_____3. It is easier for adults to learn to do a familiar task in an unfamiliar way than it is to learn a completely new task.

_____4. When learning something new, adults will take more risks than children.

Here are the answers.

1. True. Adults can't be forced or tricked into learning something new (threats and gold stars notwithstanding). They enter into—even seek out—learning experiences in order to cope with specific life-changing events, such as getting and surviving that first teaching job. Adults will engage willingly in learning activities that promise to help them with the transition. To your mentee, learning is a means to an end, not an end in itself.

2. True. The rate of learning increases with age. Learners need to integrate new ideas with what they already know. Incoming data get processed through the filter of experience, and adults have had more experiences than children. Also, information that conflicts with or has little in common with what adults already know is integrated by them more slowly. In contrast with children, adults find that fast-paced, complex learning situations interfere with the integration of new information—especially when the new material forces a reevaluation of what they already know.

(Continued)

(Continued)

3. False. You *can* teach old dogs new tricks; it's teaching them new ways to do old tricks that's the problem. New information that has little relationship to an individual's experience or behavior does not have to be filtered through very much before being added to that person's repertoire. On the other hand, a learner finds it much more difficult to integrate new information into a task that is already familiar. Like most adults, your mentee has acquired a large repertoire of behaviors and has practiced them over a long period of time. Consequently, you need to interact with your mentee with a little more patience and creativity than you might be willing to do with a child.

4. False. As a result of years of experience, adults tend to avoid venturing into trial-and-error territory and opt rather for "safe" assumptions and accurate solutions when mucking around in learning situations. Also, adults tend to let making a mistake affect their self-esteem; therefore, they usually stick to the tried and true.

FEEDBACK

The development of new skills and integration of new knowledge require time, focused effort, application, and feedback. Feedback is a form of communication that provides information to a person about the effect of that person's decisions and actions. Your mentee's development is dependent on your confirming feedback.

Criteria for Giving Useful Feedback

1. It is descriptive rather than evaluative. By describing one's own reaction, it leaves the other person free to use it as he or she sees fit. By avoiding evaluative language, it reduces the need for the individual to react defensively.

2. It is specific rather than general. To be told that one is "dominating" will probably not be as useful as to be told that "just a moment ago, as we were deciding the issue, you kept

interrupting me and I felt forced to accept your arguments or face attack from you."

3. It takes into account the needs of both the receiver and giver of feedback. Feedback can be destructive when it serves only our own needs and fails to consider the needs of the person on the receiving end.

4. It is directed toward behavior that the receiver can do something about. Frustration is only increased when a person is reminded of some shortcoming over which he or she has no control.

5. It is solicited, rather than imposed. Feedback is most useful when the receiver has formulated the kind of question that an observer can answer.

6. It is well-timed. In general, feedback is most useful at the earliest opportunity after the given behavior (depending, of course, on the person's readiness to hear it).

7. It is checked to ensure clear communication. One way of doing this is to have the receiver try to rephrase the feedback received to see if it corresponds to what the sender had in mind.

Criteria for Receiving Feedback

You can help your mentee get the most out of the pre- and post-observation conferences by providing him or her with these guidelines for receiving your feedback:

- Focus on what is being said rather than how it is said.
- Focus on feedback as information rather than criticism.
- Concentrate on receiving the new information rather than defending the old.
- Ask for specifics rather than accept generalities.
- Focus on clarifying what has been said by summarizing the main points to the satisfaction of both parties.

In summary, coaching's primary objective is to get the mentee to clarify what, when, and how to teach; to reflect on the results of those decisions; and to develop and carry out alternatives that will improve upon past performance.

CHAPTER FOUR

Guiding

W*ebster's Third New International Dictionary of the English Language, Unabridged* defines *guide* as "vb . . . to direct or supervise esp [*sic*] toward some desirable end, course, way, or development."

You function as a guide when you systematically direct or supervise your mentee's journey from unseasoned neophyte to self-reliant practitioner. Your purpose as a guide is to bring your mentee to the point where a mentor is no longer necessary, to wean your mentee away from dependence, and facilitate his or her journey toward becoming an autonomous teacher.

You establish the groundwork for this journey right from the beginning of your mentor-mentee relationship. When you legitimize and value your mentee's thoughts and feelings, in effect you are taking his or her hand; when you include your mentee in decisions about collecting and assessing data to determine needs, in effect you are gathering resources for the journey; when you ask your mentee to reflect on his or her professional decisions and actions, in effect you are charting the course; and when you encourage your mentee to construct ways to improve his or her teaching, in effect you are opening new avenues to explore.

GUIDING YOUR MENTEE'S JOURNEY: A DECISION-MAKING PROCESS

Guiding is the mentoring function that is directly concerned with the ongoing professional development of the mentee. In the process of guiding your mentee's professional development journey, you will need to make decisions along the way as to which relating and coaching behaviors will be the most appropriate to use in the various situations you will encounter. These behaviors, or strategies, will not only be those that resonate with the mentee's developmental stage at the time, but will also include those that encourage him or her to strive toward the next-higher level. In order to make such decisions, you need to look at each situation or problem being faced by your mentee in terms of (1) his or her willingness to address it and (2) his or her ability to handle or solve it.

As a general rule of thumb, you decide the *coaching* strategies to use in a given situation based on your assessment of the mentee's level of skills, knowledge, and understanding. You decide the *relating* strategies to use in a given situation based on your *assessment* of your mentee's level of willingness and motivation and his or her readiness to move on. But first you need to identify and clarify your mentee's situation or problem.

Identifying Your Mentee's Problems

There are several ways to find out what professionally related problems your mentee is facing. For instance, it is safe to assume—as Chapter 2, "Assessing," reminds us—that your mentee will share many of the concerns experienced by most beginning teachers.

A direct way to identify a problem specific to your mentee is to go into the classroom and observe its dynamics. Look for clues that tell you what your mentee is doing well, as well as what he or she doesn't know how to do very well. Also look for an indication that your mentee may know something is not going well, but is not motivated enough to try to correct the situation.

Suppose, for example, that your mentee is Dara. You notice that LaShauna, a student in Dara's class, has fallen asleep during a lesson you are observing. After class, you mention the situation to Dara, who tells you that LaShauna often dozes off in class and consequently is falling behind academically. Dara goes on to say, "LaShauna is not a good student anyhow, and because the other students do not seem to be bothered by her behavior, I'll just let sleeping dogs lie." Obviously, you have identified a problem to work on with Dara. It seems that she is not very motivated to do anything about the situation, and chances are that either she does not really understand the need to address it, or she does understand but does not know how to deal with it.

Another way to identify an area of concern is to ask your mentee to reflect on the professional issues he or she is currently experiencing. If there is a difference between the way these issues are unfolding and the way he or she (or you, for that matter) would like them to unfold—and that difference bothers either of you enough to want to do something about it—you probably have identified a significant problem.

When I was enrolled in the EdD program at the University of Massachusetts, I had the good fortune to have had Kenneth Blanchard on my doctoral committee and to have participated in two of his organizational behavior courses. These experiences gave me the opportunity to discover and internalize the Situational Leadership theory developed by Hersey and Blanchard (1974). The following guiding principles and set of scenarios are based on the Hersey and Blanchard Situational Leadership model.

GUIDING PRINCIPLES

Once you have identified and clarified your mentee's problem area, you are ready to apply these principles:

1. Determine your mentee's motivation and ability to address the problem.

2. Use coaching and relating behaviors that are appropriate to the situation. In general, the less willingness or confidence your mentee exhibits when dealing with a particular situation, the more you need to use relating and reinforcing behaviors. The less knowledge, understanding, and skill your mentee brings to the situation or problem, the more you need to structure your coaching strategies.

3. Use coaching and relating behaviors that *raise the bar*, that challenge the mentee to grow professionally.

4. Monitor your mentee's progress, and vary your behaviors accordingly.

Following are a set of scenarios that apply these principles. The vignettes chronicle four events involving James, a beginning teacher, that take place during his first year. Each episode finds James in a different situation, and each situation requires a different kind of mentoring behavior—a different kind of guidance.

THE UNWILLING AND UNABLE MENTEE

It is the beginning of a school year and you are mentoring James, a first-year teacher. James has passed State University's rigid and comprehensive teacher preparation program, and he clearly knows his subject matter. He is a bright young man, but a bit shy.

During an early observation of his classroom, it is evident that James is having difficulty managing student discipline. His attempts to entice and inveigle students into behaving are having little success.

After class, James says to you, "Did you see Jimmy throw that paper clip?"

You nod.

His gaze shifts toward the floor. "I wish the other students hadn't made such a big deal about it."

You note that James's eyes lowered to his right and that he used the words, "I wish." Because both of these reactions are clues that he is in a feeling sensory mode, you ask:

"You feel as though the students are being disruptive?"

"Yes. Their acting out is interfering with my teaching. I'm not sure that I can turn things around. I've tried. It's very discouraging."

Your assessment of James's classroom discipline problem indicates that he needs help on two levels: He needs the skills to solve the problem and the willingness and confidence to tackle it. What do you do?

Coaching Strategies

The immediacy of this situation and James's obvious need for structure call for a *show-and-tell* style of coaching. "This is what to do, James," you tell him. "Rearrange seating [show him how]; establish and maintain rules and standards of behavior [give him a list]; avoid using sarcasm; don't plead for attention; show enthusiasm for the content and for learning; and announce and apply consequences for inappropriate student behavior [give him a list of such consequences]." You are encouraged when James looks at your list of punishments for students not following rules and asks, "Shouldn't there be positive consequences for appropriate behavior?"

Invite James to observe one of your classes to see how you manage discipline. Give him a copy of Harry and Rosemary Wong's (1999) *First Days of School* to read and point out specific strategies. If appropriate, arrange for him to observe another teacher's class management techniques.

Relating Strategies

You will need to strengthen and support James's willingness and motivation to apply your suggestions. You cannot "motivate" someone else. Motivation is self-constructed. The extent to which a mentee is willing to take some action is influenced by what he or she perceives as important and what he or she believes can be accomplished. The more a situation affects one's values and the higher one's expectations of success, the stronger the motivation.

Given James's seeming lack of motivation to work out his own classroom management problem, you should (1) increase expectations of success and (2) encourage his sense of responsibility. These strategies are especially important because they are germane to helping James become a self-reliant teacher.

Here are some specific ways to support James and enhance his self-confidence.

Set short-term, realistic goals. For example, tell James to try out the techniques you shared with him for the next three days, after which you will meet to discuss what happened and what to do next.

Acknowledge James's efforts and validate his ideas. Be honest and specific. For example, tell him that he showed insight when he suggested adding rewards for appropriate behavior to your list of consequences.

You can also support James by defusing any unjust criticism from others and by providing resources that will help him carry out the new strategies.

In general, when your mentee is both unmotivated and unable to deal with a situation, your coaching and relating strategies should focus on behaviors that will fix that particular problem. However, soon thereafter, it is important to switch to a reflecting style of coaching and place responsibility once again on the mentee.

THE MODERATELY WILLING AND SOMEWHAT ABLE MENTEE

It is a week later, and James is working hard on his class management problem. It is still not quite under control, but there are signs of improvement. At the end of a conversation about the situation, James says to you, "I've been thinking of changing the way I had planned to teach a particular unit, but I'm uncertain about some of the details. Can we discuss my ideas?"

You are elated. By the nature of his statement, James has indicated his readiness and willingness to approach *this* situation by sharing ideas and exploring new strategies together. In other words, your assessment of James's sense of competency and confidence in this instance suggests that he would prefer to work in collaboration with his mentor and contribute to discussions—clearly a different level of ability and motivation from what he exhibited in the discipline scenario. James's words and attitude show that he is willing to take responsibility for clarifying concepts about teaching and learning and to share in the making of informed decisions. What do you do?

Coaching Strategies

Your strategy in this situation is to encourage James to reflect on his ideas. Ask him probing, open-ended questions, such as, "How do you see this new activity engaging students more powerfully than the one you had planned to use?" This is also an opportunity for you both to brainstorm for alternative strategies and to discuss possible resources. When you and James have agreed on a particular new approach, encourage him to try it out and see what happens. Offer to observe that class—or suggest that James have the class video-recorded—and to meet with him afterward to discuss and fine-tune the outcome. During that postobservation meeting, you might say something like, "We both agree that the new activity went well and that most of the students grasped the concept rather quickly. I noticed, however, that the new activity left some of the students so stimulated that it took them a long time to get into the next activity. Let's brainstorm ways that might have helped those students settle down more quickly. (Hand him a professional journal.) Try to make time during the week to read the articles in this journal and see what research has to offer in the way of suggestions."

Your follow-up strategy is to continue to encourage and help James find and use resources, human and otherwise; make informed decisions; take some considered risks; and reflect on the outcomes of those actions.

As James becomes more competent, you gradually offer less direction and cooperation and begin to encourage James to try out and evaluate his own ideas, letting him know that you are interested in hearing about them and how they are working.

Relating Strategies

Listen to James's ideas. Let him know you are paying attention. Do this through the use of body language and by paraphrasing back to him what you understood him to have said.

Celebrate James's successes by sending his principal or supervisor a note (copied to James) commending James's initiative and citing any resultant improvement in student learning.

Let James know that you appreciated having been asked to discuss his ideas. Offer to look over and provide feedback on other ideas he might have.

Give James an opportunity for some guided practice by offering to help him revise curriculum or other lesson plans.

THE COMPETENT AND CONFIDENT MENTEE

It is the first day back from spring vacation. You pass James in the hall, return his smile, and nod your greetings to each other. What a change from the beginning of the school year when James was having so much trouble with student discipline! Now, when it comes to maintaining a productive classroom climate, James is a master. He is sensitive to subtle shifts in student attention, is able to orchestrate and focus student participation, and has the flexibility to recognize and take advantage of teachable moments. As a mentor, what do you do?

Coaching and Relating Strategies

Honor James's strength in this area by not interfering. You might let him know that you recognize his success. Suggest that he outline his strategies so that he can share his techniques with his colleagues in some way, perhaps by leading an informal discussion around the topic.

THE ALL-OF-THE-ABOVE MENTEE

Chances are that your mentee will be at different stages of ability and motivation in various teaching scenarios. As we have just seen, for example, James has acquired a great deal of competence and confidence in establishing rapport with students. He is also adept at maintaining an effective classroom climate. Obviously, he now needs very little mentoring in these areas.

In another regard, James tells you that he is pleased with the way his lesson-planning ability has improved since the beginning of the year. He also lets you know that he has taken up the challenge of continuing to improve in that area. Your appropriate mentoring style now is to provide collaboration and encouragement rather than offering specific suggestions or adopting a *hands-off* attitude.

Exercise 4.1   Help James Assess His Students

Suppose you notice that James often takes it for granted that students understand the material he presents. As a result, he gets frustrated and discouraged when student test results fail to support his estimation of the students' understanding. What would you do? What relating and coaching behaviors are appropriate? Write your ideas below.

_____

_____

_____

_____

(Continued)

(Continued)

> *Discussion:* You could have written a variety of appropriate behaviors. In general, structured coaching strategies and objective, nonjudgmental listening behaviors are called for here. Coaching behaviors that respond to James's need to clarify and restructure his student assessment efforts are appropriate. He also needs relating behaviors from you that will help him resolve the emotional issues connected with the pedagogical ones. Do the strategies you listed satisfy these requirements?

In the above scenarios, we see that a mentee can exhibit the need for different mentoring strategies in different situations at relatively the same time. You are a successful mentor in these scenarios not only because you exhibit good coaching, relating, and guiding skills, but also because you assess and diagnose effectively, you are flexible, and you are able to use appropriate behaviors in a variety of given situations.

Exercise 4.2   Practice Choosing the Appropriate Behavior

In this exercise, you will have the opportunity to practice your diagnostic skills. For each situation below, there are four alternative behaviors. Decide on the most appropriate behavior for that situation.

Situation 1: You and your mentee, Lois, have been getting along well; in fact, you have become good friends. Professionally, you have recently switched from a structured to a looser reflecting style of coaching to help Lois improve her ability to develop lesson plans. You started originally with a show-and-tell style because Lois exhibited few lesson-planning skills at the time. Progress has been slow but steady. Recently, however, Lois's interest in improving has waned, and her lesson-planning ability has regressed back to the point where it is almost nonexistent. What would you do?

   a. Switch back to show-and-tell coaching
   b. Discuss the situation with Lois and mutually agree on a solution

c. Continue using a reflective style, but let Lois know you are concerned

d. Remain friendly on a personal level, but adopt a hands-off posture professionally

Discussion: The most appropriate immediate behavior is *a.* You need to get Lois back on track in a hurry. When she begins to show signs of willingness to resume some responsibility, you can let up a bit and go to a more collaborative style such as *b.* Alternative *c* holds little promise until motivation increases. Alternative *d* will only make the situation worse, because Lois does not have the skills to improve on her own.

Situation 2: Your and your mentee, Sam, have worked together to establish an effective and supportive classroom climate. Your successful coaching behavior was to ask probing questions that encouraged Sam to reflect and to construct his own classroom strategies. Until recently, Sam has experienced no major discipline problems. However, one student has begun to act out, and Sam has been unable to control the boy's continuous disruptive behavior. Sam asks you for help. What would you do?

a. Go into Sam's classroom and deal with the disruptive student yourself

b. Encourage Sam to work out a solution himself

c. Brainstorm some ideas with Sam, let him try some out, and meet later to reflect on their effectiveness

d. Listen to Sam's ideas about how to solve the problem and give him feedback

Discussion: The most appropriate behavior is *c.* Sam has shown the willingness and ability to work on classroom discipline with you in the past, and for the most part has been able to do so successfully on his own since then. However, he has asked for your help in this instance. You can best help by revisiting with him the behaviors that worked before. Alternative *a* is not only an overreaction, it also undermines Sam's rapport with his class. Alternatives *b* and *d* are inappropriate because

(Continued)

(Continued)

Sam has already tried and been unsuccessful; he does need some help and is wise enough to ask. Once the problem is solved, you no longer need to be involved.

Situation 3: You are an experienced physical education teacher in a small school district. A new state mandate requires a change in the physical education curriculum. Jane was hired this year as the district's only other physical education teacher. You are Jane's mentor. Since the opening day of the school year, Jane has handled responsibility extremely well. She also has exhibited an excellent understanding of her subject and how to teach it. Jane agrees with the state mandate and respects the need for curriculum revision. Although she has no previous experience with curriculum revision, Jane is very good at tracking down information when she needs to. What would you do?

 a. Oversee the curriculum revision, but allow Jane considerable involvement and input
 b. Delegate to Jane the authority and responsibility for the revision
 c. Revise the curriculum yourself and make sure Jane understands and follows it
 d. Revise the curriculum, but ask for Jane's recommendations

Discussion: The most appropriate behavior is *b.* Jane is knowledgeable and highly motivated in regard to this situation and needs little intervention from you other than some resources, proofreading, and perhaps a little help with formatting a curriculum document. Because the revised curriculum will be "her baby," Jane will be very likely to follow it, reflect on its implementation, and upgrade it as needed. Delegating this responsibility to Jane not only will validate her professionalism, it will also move her toward becoming even more self-reliant. Alternative *a* would be the appropriate choice if you have legitimate doubts about Jane's ability in the area of curriculum development and feel that she needs direction in this regard. Alternative *d* does not take full advantage of—nor does it honor—Jane's potential. Alternative *c* not only ignores Jane's competence and confidence, it also undermines the mentor-mentee relationship by eroding trust.

Situation 4: As a first-year teacher, Michael, your mentee, is doing well in the classroom. Recently, however, he has become a nonconformist when it comes to following school policy and paying attention to everyday procedures. Some of the staff and other teachers are getting annoyed with Michael because they perceive that his behavior will soon cause problems. When you point this situation out to Michael, he tells you that he will try to pay more attention to policies and procedures, but after a week or two, there is no change. What would you do?

    a. Keep a low profile, allow Michael to experience the consequences of his behavior, and let him take responsibility for working out his own problems

    b. Insist that Michael follow the rules and keep close tabs on his behavior

    c. Ask Michael how he will deal with the situation and offer your help and advice

    d. Redefine and clarify for Michael the expectations and responsibilities having to do with policies and procedures, monitor his progress, and reinforce positive behavior

Discussion: The most appropriate behavior is *d*. Michael needs to understand and appreciate the rationale behind the school's policies and procedures and take responsibility for adhering to them. This situation initially calls for a structured rather than reflective coaching behavior, coupled with an attentive and supportive relationship style. Alternative *a* will only increase the probability that the behavior will continue, and possibly worsen. Alternative *b* is too drastic in that it ignores the need for increased motivation and will probably have an adverse effect on the mentor-mentee relationship as well. Alternative *c* asks the unmotivated mentee to make an uninformed decision.

Situation 5: Alejandro, your mentee, tells you that he is uncomfortable with the way he had planned to teach the cells-and-genes unit of his general biology class. He has a few ideas about how he might approach the unit differently and has asked you to help him decide which one to use. What would you do?

(Continued)

(Continued)

> a. Hear Alejandro's ideas, tell him which one seems to have the most merit, and thank him for asking for your help
> b. Get Alejandro to reflect on his alternative ideas, perhaps generate new ones together, agree on the one to try, and arrange to discuss the results
> c. Ask Alejandro to describe his original plan, listen attentively to his alternate ideas, validate his feelings, then encourage him to decide for himself which idea to use
> d. Listen to what Alejandro has to say, then share with him a solution that works for you in such a situation and suggest he use it too
>
> *Discussion:* Alternatives *a*, *b*, and *c* each pay attention to the relationship, but it is behavior *b* that responds best to Alejandro's readiness for a collaborative style of coaching. Alternative *a* takes care of Alejandro's request to help him make up his mind, but misses the opportunity to help him develop his problem-solving skills. Alternative *c* ignores the probability that Alejandro's competence is not yet strong enough to support a confident decision. Alternative *d* disregards Alejandro's readiness for collaboration.

FROM MENTOR-MENTEE TO PEER-PEER

The purpose of the guiding function is to wean your mentee away from relying on you for direction and suggestions. The goal is to make your role as mentor (to this mentee) no longer necessary. You will know you have achieved this goal when your mentee demonstrates the willingness and ability to make informed professional decisions autonomously, act on those decisions with confidence, reflect on the effectiveness of those actions, and modify procedures based on thoughtful analysis of accurate data. At this point—usually by the middle of the second or start of the third year of teaching—the status of your collegial relationship will have transformed from mentor-mentee to peer-peer, a partnership in which you each function as a mentor for the other.

CHAPTER FIVE

Mentoring's Legacy

Career-Long Professional Development

Dennis Sparks, executive director emeritus of the National Staff Development Association, points out that mentors "provide beginning teachers with their introduction to career-long . . . professional development through which they continuously improve their teaching and student learning" (Sparks, 2005, p. 241). Yes, effective mentoring is a potent introduction to career-long professional development, and mentors must recognize and attend to their responsibility in this area. But mentoring is only an introduction. Over the years, schools, districts, state departments of education, and consulting firms will probably provide a myriad of professional development opportunities. Ultimately, however, it will be the individual teacher that must become the steward of the direction and effectiveness of his or her own ongoing professional growth. Dennis Sparks' assertion suggests to me that effective mentoring includes preparing new teachers to take responsibility for their own career-long professional growth.

TEACHER'S INQUIRY PROCESS

Many of today's young teachers are output-driven and achievement-oriented. They want what they do to have meaning and to be effective. Most want and value clear rules and procedures and respond well to structure (Alsop, 2006). Consequently, I have conceptualized and applied the Teacher's Inquiry Process (TIP). TIP is intended to develop a teacher's capacity and confidence to take responsibility for and control of his or her own professional development. If you are a mentor, I encourage you to use TIP with your mentee. TIP uses data and reflection to identify and focus on a specific professional need. It then prompts the generation of activities to address that need, then goes on to elicit details to help activate those activities. Before I describe TIP itself, here are its caveats and ground rules.

TIP is not a plan. It is a planning process—a guide designed to stimulate critical and creative thinking that leads to action-based decisions.

Teachers have more than enough paperwork with which to contend. TIP is not *paperwork* to be handed in or filed. Rather, it consists of a series of prompts to stimulate and guide personal or group reflection—either spoken or written. It has no official status, and except for possible inclusion in one's journal or portfolio, it need not be documented.

TIP is an eight-step process. It is not meant to be completed all at once. TIP is best applied over time, concentrating on one or two steps—or even part of one step—during each session. It may be necessary for the whole process to extend over a week or two, but it shouldn't be stretched out much longer than that.

Initially, TIP takes place in cooperation between mentees and their mentors. TIP can also be used by a cohort of beginning teachers and their mentors or facilitators who can bounce ideas off of each other. Mentors use a process comparable to a postobservation conference. They challenge their mentees to look deeper and harder—to go places they otherwise may not think about or even be willing to think about. By going through TIP with their mentors and/or their peers, novices hear their own thoughts aloud, along with verbal inflections and intonations that suggest meaning beyond the words. In addition, there is the opportunity to elicit and receive feedback that is informed by experiences, knowledge, and beliefs different from their own and therefore has the potential to provide new insights. Eventually, the teacher can continue to use TIP in collaboration with others or decide to go through the process alone.

The ultimate purpose of TIP is to improve teaching and learning. When teachers reflect on their professional practice with the objective of learning to teach better, the teacher and learner are the same person. Read the previous sentence again; it has very powerful implications. It means that TIP provides a way to mentor oneself and thereby monitor one's own professional growth.

Some school districts require that teachers develop and carry out individualized professional development plans. In such cases, teachers will probably need to use standard forms, keep records, and follow certain procedures. They can still benefit from TIP, however, because it generates decisions on how and when to carry out specific activities that may relate to goals called for in official individual plans. Check with the person in your school district responsible for professional development, personnel, or human resources to determine whether your state and local policies allow focused independent study such as TIP to earn continuing education units, professional development points, or other recertification points.

TIP is most effective when it concentrates on one designated and defined outcome, rather than on a general category or need. Because TIP focuses on addressing a specific desired outcome, it allows for tweaking and adjusting where appropriate. It also generates benchmarks that, when met, provide a clear sense of accomplishment.

The best time to introduce TIP to mentees is toward the end of their first year or shortly after the start of year two. These are good times because there will be a year's supply of memories, reflections, and data still fresh in the mentees' minds and at their fingertips.

There are intangible benefits associated with TIP, not the least of which is that when informed by data, the input of others, and reflection, mentees become professionals who decide for themselves what to work on, how to work on it, and when to work on it. TIP users set their own schedules, select their own resources, and determine their own activities and desired outcomes. They decide for themselves whether to use TIP throughout their careers, and if so, to do so either on their own or in collaboration with others.

Most importantly, TIP is designed to address the *big question*: ***What do I need to know and be able to do, that I don't know or can't do now, in order to better help my students achieve what they need to know and be able to do?***

TIP in Action

The following scenario is a fabricated example of a typical application of TIP. It illustrates how a mentor—let's call her Annette—mentored Gerry, a new middle school history teacher, through TIP's eight steps.

Gerry is a little more than one month into his second year as a teacher. Last year, fresh out of college, Gerry received positive evaluations from his principal, and overall, he experienced a successful first year—except for his ancient world history class. He is teaching that class again this year and is having similar concerns about its effectiveness. Annette, his mentor, feels that Gerry is ready to take responsibility for determining what he needs to know and be able to do in order to make the class more successful. Gerry and Annette agree to use TIP for this purpose. Following is an account of the eight TIP steps undertaken by Gerry with facilitation by his mentor.

Step 1. Analyze and reflect on data and insights gathered during postobservation conferences and similar interactions with your mentor and others to identify a specific area of concern where there is a difference between the way things are and the way you would like them to be.

Annette: What is the most enjoyable aspect of your teaching, Gerry?

Gerry: Seeing my students get involved in class projects because they are really getting into the work. I love seeing them find a way to hook into what we're studying. It's very gratifying to know they are learning and that they enjoy doing so.

Annette: If you had to describe in one sentence how you know whether your students are learning, what would you say?

Gerry: I know my students are learning when they can show me they mastered the objectives of the lesson by applying the concepts in a project and getting correct answers on tests.

Annette: You expressed concern about your ancient world history class. According to criteria you just expressed, are the students in your ancient world history class learning to your satisfaction?

Gerry: No.

Annette: Tell me more. Other than passing tests, what do you want them to get out of class that they are not getting now?

Gerry: Well, I want my students to be critical, engaged, active citizens prepared to participate in a democratic society. I also want them to know salient aspects of ancient cultures and ways in which contemporary life has evolved form those cultures. But they just don't seem to get the connection. They just go through the motions and their test scores are horrible. I really would like them to understand that ancient world history is relevant to their lives, but I don't seem to be able to get them to do so. Instead, I get comments like "Why do we have to learn this?"

Annette: I know that you have used several strategies designed to make connections between ancient and contemporary life. For example, I recall that you had students identify on a map which modern countries used to be under the control of the Roman empire and explain how these countries have been influenced by ancient Rome.

Gerry: Yes, that one worked out OK. Another thing I've tried is assigning an end-of-unit paper explaining how three aspects of the civilization we studied have affected our lives. They didn't do well on that assignment, but they did have fun with another one where they dressed up in togas for an activity where they role played that they were teenagers in ancient Rome. I pulled a pop quiz at the end of the activity.

Annette: And . . . ?

Gerry: I guess they were motivated to have fun, but not to learn the material. I really believe they would be motivated to learn if I could get them to connect ancient world history to their own lives.

Annette: We can talk more about that toga activity another time, but for now, it seems you feel that you need to find better ways to teach the curriculum in ways that motivate students to understand the material in terms of their own lives.

Gerry: Exactly!

Annette: Would you say that there is a difference between the way things are in that class and the way you would like them to be, *and that difference bothers you professionally*?"

Gerry: Absolutely. It bothers me quite a bit.

Step 2. Using the present tense, describe the situation as though everything was going well and the concern did not exist. What do you see, hear, smell, taste, feel in this ideal setting? What are others saying and doing? What are you saying and doing?

Annette: Imagine that your students are motivated and are fully engaged in the class. Using present tense, Gerry, can you describe to me what is happening in such an ideal classroom? What are students saying and doing? What are you saying and doing?

Gerry (smiling):   My students are enthusiastically raising their hands and offering examples of how ancient Rome relates to their lives. They are explaining how ancient Rome matters because our government is based on those principles, and they accurately express this in tests. I am encouraging them to talk about issues in ancient Rome much the way people their age today would speak out about their opinions. They are really getting into it, and their test scores show it.

Step 3. As specifically as you can, describe the concern you want to address. Write your thoughts in the form of a series of reflective questions and statements. Limit your focus to one particular concern.

Gerry writes: How can I make ancient world history relevant to my students? What does *relevant* mean? How can I measure relevancy? How can I help my students connect ancient world history to their lives? How can I help them to see that history matters in our world today? How can I get students to make connections between ancient civilizations and our world today, especially in terms of their own lives?

Step 4. Identify gaps in your abilities, knowledge, skills, understandings, and/or resources that may be keeping you from addressing your concern.

Annette: From what you wrote, Gerry, I get the sense that you would like to come up with activities that will help students make those connections.

Gerry: Right. I need to create some projects. It might be a good idea to find out what other teachers have done.

Annette: Sounds like a good idea. What about your students? Do you know what their interests are that could connect with ancient times?

Gerry: I could find out about their hobbies.

Step 5. Identify potential resources that can inform your inquiry.

Annette: Your next step, Gerry, is to consider what resources are out there. At our last meeting, you thought it might be a good idea to find out what other teachers are doing. That would be a good place to start.

Gerry: I will talk with and arrange to observe my colleagues. Also, I meet with members of my team on a regular basis, and I participate in a new teacher's group every other week. I'm sure they would have some good ideas.

Annette: Excellent. There is a lot of other help out there, too. For example, the Internet is a good resource. You can use a search engine like Google or Yahoo! Enter a key word or phrase, such as *impact of ancient history on today's youth*, and follow the promising links it will offer. And you can post your questions and concerns on Internet chatboards such as those on http://teachers.net. Another good source is the Education Resources Information Center (ERIC), which you can search for articles having to do with your topic. The librarian can help you with this. University faculty, publications, professional organizations, regional and state education agencies—even your family and friends—are other potential resources.

Gerry: Great suggestions. Thanks. I can also find out what the district plans to offer in the way of professional development activities that relate to my concern. And I heard that Yahoo.com and HotChalk.com offer a free online service for educators to create, find, and share lesson plans, worksheets, and ideas.

Step 6. List specific actions you will undertake to fill or bridge the gaps you have identified. Estimate a start and end date for each action.

Annette: Let's talk about specific activities that you will do. What can be your first steps?

Gerry: I will bring my concern to the new teachers' group. We meet tomorrow afternoon. I can also search on-line for lesson plans.

Annette: Cool. Let's write down activities and time lines. It will serve as a handy reminder and checklist. You will have the satisfaction of crossing off each activity as it is completed. Occasionally you may find it necessary to modify, add to, or omit some activities you've listed. By all means do so, but be careful not to compromise the basic intent and integrity of your inquiry and area of concern in the process.

Here is Gerry's list:

Activity	Estimated Start Date	Estimated End Date
Research lesson plans and articles on Internet (Google & Yahoo!).	10/16	10/27
Present concern to team and new teachers' group.	10/17	12/8
Talk with and observe Mrs. Vasquez and Mr. Carlson.	10/23	11/2
Develop two lessons/units and review them with my team and new teachers' group.	11/3	11/16

Teach new lessons/units.	11/27	12/14
Ask Annette to observe and give feedback.		
Review and modify as indicated.	12/18	1/12
Repeat above steps. Modify as needed.	1/12	5/18

Step 7. Commit to carrying out the activities.

Annette: Completing these activities will take time, effort, and stretching, Gerry. Can you honestly say that the activities are achievable and worthwhile; that they represent a worthy challenge?

Gerry: Yes, I can. As I said when we began this process, I want my students to get involved in class projects. I love seeing them find a way to hook into what we're studying. It would be very gratifying to know they are learning and that they enjoy doing so.

Annette: I hear and appreciate your enthusiasm and commitment, Gerry. I'll be looking forward to hearing about your progress, but remember, this is your project. I'm always ready to help wherever I can, so please let me know if you would like to discuss any issue.

Step 8. Assess the results.
These are the questions Annette asked Gerry in Step 8:

- Did you complete the activities? (If not, why not?)
- (If yes) Did you apply what you learned? What was the result? (If you did not apply what you learned, why not?)

Gerry did apply what he learned and with positive results. From discussions with his team and new teachers' group, he organized units to connect history to history (e.g., Compare the way Romans lived to the way other ancient civilizations lived); history to self (e.g., Write a journal of your life as if it were happening in ancient Rome); and history with today's world (e.g., Compare and contrast ancient governments with contemporary ones).

Gerry also learned that many of his students were interested in sports. On the HotChalk Lesson Plans (MyLibrary) Web page, he found and successfully adapted a lesson plan titled the "History of the Olympics" (Senigo, 2001) with these objectives:

- The students will research the history of the Olympics.
- The students will discuss and present the changes in the Olympics from ancient Greek times to present day.
- The students will use their knowledge of the Olympics to design their own rules and hold their own Olympics.

Gerry's imagined ideal class had come to pass!

TIP's Eight Steps: A Summary

Step 1. Analyze and reflect on data and insights gathered during postobservation conferences and similar interactions with your mentor and others to identify a specific area of concern where there is a difference between the way things are and the way you would like them to be.

Step 2. Using the present tense, describe the situation as though everything was going well and the concern did not exist. What do you see, hear, smell, taste, feel in this ideal setting? What are others saying and doing? What are you saying and doing?

Step 3. As specifically as you can, describe the concern you want to address. Write your thoughts in the form of a series of reflective questions and statements. Limit your focus to one particular concern.

Step 4. Identify gaps in your abilities, knowledge, skills, understandings, and/or resources that may be keeping you from addressing your concern.

Step 5. Identify potential resources that can inform your inquiry.

Step 6. List specific actions you will undertake to fill or bridge the gaps you identified. Estimate a start and end date for each action.

Step 7. Commit to carrying out the activities.

Step 8. Assess the results.

FROM TIP TO MIP

I modified TIP for use in advanced mentoring workshops for experienced mentors. Mentors can use it to as a guide to taking charge of their own development as mentors. See Resource D for the Mentor Inquiry Process (MIP).

Chapter Six

Tips and Observations

Set Ground Rules Early

At the beginning of your association with a mentee, discuss the objectives of the relationship. Sort out roles, boundaries, expectations, and processes. Clarify issues of confidentiality. If there is disagreement, or if you do not know the answer to a question, present your position and feelings honestly so that there will be no false assumptions.

Help Change Happen

If you are thwarted in attempts to bring about a change in your mentee or in the mentoring process, try the following:

1. Define the desired change using specific, measurable terms.
2. List everything you can think of that is resisting or getting in the way of that change.
3. List everything you can think of that is helping or can help that change take place.
4. Develop strategies to intensify items that help, dilute items that hinder, and change resisting items into supporting ones.

Avoid Information Overload

Provide information and material to your mentee as needed. Don't saturate him or her with particulars months, weeks, or even days before there is a need to know them; the minutiae will get filtered out in favor of more immediate needs. For example, delay a discussion of parent-teacher meeting protocol until shortly before any meetings are scheduled to take place.

SHARE DECISION MAKING

When you have identified a mentee's need, don't assume that he or she agrees with you. Work together on identifying needs. Reach agreement concerning what to work on.

KNOW WHEN TO INTERVENE

Know when to step in and when to stand back from a touchy situation. Intervene when a situation threatens someone's health and safety. Intervene if your mentee has failed in several attempts to handle a problem and specifically asks for your intervention. Avoid intervening when doing so will detract from your mentee's credibility. Consider whether intervening will keep your mentee from an opportunity to learn and grow.

MENTORING, REMEDIATING, AND PEER REVIEW

You may be called upon to work with or mentor another veteran teacher, one whose performance has been evaluated as being below par. Much of the material in this book can apply in such a situation. However, if you are expected to *remediate* the mentee, mentoring is not what will be going on. Being mentored means you are developing the capacity to fix yourself; being remediated means someone else is fixing you. In addition, if you are expected to *evaluate* the other teacher, the vital element of trust so necessary in a mentor/mentee relationship is likely to be compromised. In this situation, your focus should not be on mentoring, but on assistance; not on assessing your colleague's competency, but rather on helping the teacher prepare for assessment by someone else.

Suppose you are asked to submit a written report on your mentee's progress. You can honor that request, but in that report, you want to make it clear—either directly or through implication—that your role as a mentor precludes you from formally evaluating your mentee. You should share the report with your mentee, not only for his or her information, but also in order to reinforce the trust and confidentiality of the mentor-mentee relationship. For example, a phrase you might use in such a report is, "My role as mentor is to facilitate_____'s efforts to determine and address his own professional development needs. We are involved in this process and it is progressing well."

MAINTAIN THE RELATIONSHIP

Where personalities and schedules permit, employ a medley of relationship-building opportunities with your mentee. Attend workshops and meetings together. Engage in informal chit-chat about teaching, politics, sports, or books—perhaps over coffee or lunch, or while jogging or playing golf. All too often, mentors and mentees tend to decrease their contact under the press of other demands.

DON'T FORGET CONTENT

Take every opportunity to keep your mentee up to speed on the subject he or she teaches. Encourage membership and participation in professional associations. Get your school's professional library to subscribe to relevant periodicals and acquire pertinent publications. Share and discuss the most recent national, state, and local curriculum standards. Review together and discuss the potential use of newly available technology texts and supplementary material. Also, you should check to see whether your state is a member of the Interstate New Teacher Assessment and Support Consortium (INTASC). INTASC is a program of the Council of Chief State School Officers and is concerned with teacher licensing procedures. Because INTASC is working on developing content-specific standards that will be used for assessing beginning teachers, you will want to be sure that your mentee knows of and can meet those standards. INTASC has already designed prototype assessment standards based on English, language arts, and mathematics. Others are being considered.

What Is Your Mentee Asking For?

James Rowley (2000) reminds mentors that they need to be sensitive to what mentees need from them so that they can respond appropriately. For example, are they asking for *action*, *information*, or *understanding* when they say, "The copy machine was down this morning and I have to copy my test for fifth period"? Sometimes the type of request is obvious, but it is wise not to assume. If not certain, ask.

The appropriate responses to requests for action or information are usually straightforward. A request for understanding may be more subtle. Rarely will a mentee say, "I need some understanding." Instead, they may exhibit some nonverbal clue or color their words with expressions of anger, frustration, disillusionment, or disappointment. Appropriate emotional support in response to a request for understanding may take the form of empathy, encouragement, or simply just listening. Support your mentee's need for understanding to a point, but discourage overdependence.

Know When to Wean

"Enough, already!" This is what Ms. Greene, a department chair, had to tell a mentor. The mentor had done a good job mentoring a teacher in Ms. Greene's department, but had long since passed the point where the mentee needed a mentor. The relationship had become a parent-child one. Don't become a "professional mentor." Know when to let go.

Find Time to Mentor

With luck, you and your mentee will be able to arrange ten to fifteen minutes together before and after school, during lunch or free periods, between sessions at conferences or meetings, and even during bus or cafeteria duty. Carol Pelletier (2006) illustrates what a mentor can discuss with a new teacher in blocks of time ranging from five minutes to two hours.

Yes, arranging blocks of time can present difficulties, but if mentoring is a high enough priority, you will find some way to create the time. Ideally, those who plan and administer mentoring programs will have arranged the time for you and your mentee to work together. Your district may even have received a grant to "buy" the time in the form of stipends, substitutes, or creative scheduling configurations. If not—or even if it has—here are a couple of things *you* can do.

Video-record your mentee's class (you need not be present). You will still need face-to-face pre- and postobservation conferences, but they can be scheduled more flexibly than classroom visits. You can then review the video at your convenience and use it during the conference.

Another way to free up a block of time during the school day is to make the following type of arrangement with a colleague. Together, develop a schedule for the year that combines both of your classes at regular intervals—say, once every other week. Alternate teaching the combined class. Because you will know well ahead of time when your class size will double, you can plan lessons accordingly. Be sure to get your principal's permission and cooperation.

EARN POINTS TOWARD TEACHER RECERTIFICATION

Several state departments of education require certified teachers to periodically renew their teaching credentials. Typically, teachers meet this mandate by earning a minimum number of continuing education units, professional development points, or some other indicator of time spent participating in professional development activities. Generally, documented independent study can also earn credit toward recertification.

If your state has such a mandate and you are mentoring or preparing to mentor a colleague, you may be able to apply the time you are engaged in completing the exercises in this book toward fulfilling your teaching recertification requirement. Check with the person in your school district responsible for professional development, personnel, or human resources to determine whether your state and local policies allow focused independent study, such as this book's format provides, to earn recertification points. Working through all of this book's exercises should take about ten to twelve hours.

REFLECT ON YOUR MENTORING

Keep an ongoing journal of your mentoring experience. I suggest a three-column format. Record what you did, indicate why you did it, and report what resulted. Include impressions, feelings, and anecdotes. Reflect on your journal entries and note, for example, how you might approach a particular situation differently next time. You might want to share some of your entries with your mentee. Encourage your mentee to keep a similar journal.

CONSIDER MULTIPLE MENTORS

It may be advantageous to share your mentee with another mentor. This option allows you to devote less time to the mentee and to discuss confidential issues concerning the mentee with a colleague. The use of a mentoring team can also distribute roles according to strengths, that is content, acculturation, and coaching.

BUILD A MENTORING COMMUNITY

In his article, "Preparing Mentors of Beginning Teachers: An Overview for Staff Developers," Tom Ganser (1996) warns, "designating individuals as 'official' mentors can cause other teachers, administrators, and school personnel to abdicate their professional obligation toward the beginning teacher. They may inaccurately look upon the mentor as the only person responsible for assisting the beginner rather than being an integral part of a complex process that includes them as well" (p. 9).

Sharon Daloz Parks, associate professor of pastoral theology and human development at Weston School of Theology, expanded on Ganser's admonition during a plenary address given in San Francisco at the 1990 annual meeting of the American Association of Higher Education. Parks contended, "A single mentor is sufficient for an initiation into the conventions of the corporation or the university or the society as each is presently constituted. But if one is to be initiated into a . . . more adequate . . . alternative . . . , nothing less than a mentoring community will do." She went on to say that "ongoing research makes it increasingly evident that those who are able to work on behalf of personal and social transformation are those who . . . were part of a mentoring community—a group who shared a . . . mentoring vision."

FIND NETWORKING OPPORTUNITIES

If you are the only mentor or have only one or two mentoring colleagues in your district, it is desirable that you have a support system so that you are not operating in isolation. All educators, even mentors, need inspiration and encouragement to continue to learn and grow professionally. In case your local or neighboring educational community does not provide the opportunity to interact periodically with other mentors, some professional associations offer this service. The Association for Supervision and Curriculum Development and the International Mentoring Association, for example, support mentoring networks.

REMEMBER, STUDENT LEARNING IS THE GOAL

Always keep in mind that the ultimate purpose behind your efforts to improve your mentee's teaching is to improve student learning. When assessing your mentee's needs, ask yourself, "What else does this beginning teacher need to know and be able to do in order to help students achieve what they need to know and be able to do?"

PASS THE TORCH

When your mentee has become a self-reliant teacher, give him or her this counsel: Do as I did, BECOME A MENTOR TO A NEW TEACHER!

Resource A

Teacher Mentor Standards

CORE PROPOSITIONS

Effective mentors are committed to their protégés' professional development.

Effective mentors understand how their protégés learn and act on the belief that their protégés can learn to teach better. They adjust their practice based on observation and knowledge of their protégés' interests, abilities, skills, and knowledge.

Effective mentors incorporate current research in and theories of relating, assessing, coaching/guiding, and supporting in their practice. They are aware of the influence of context and culture on behavior. They facilitate development of their protégés' instructional ability, content knowledge, and understanding of student learning.

Effective mentors know, apply, monitor, and adjust their mentoring strategies.

Effective mentors have a specialized knowledge base, honed application skills, and a varied assortment of adjustment strategies. They appreciate how knowledge in their craft is created, organized, linked to other teacher induction efforts, and applied to real-world settings.

Effective mentors understand where difficulties are likely to arise and modify their practice accordingly. Their mentoring repertoire allows them to create multiple paths to problem identification and solution. They are adept at bringing protégés to the point at which they can pose and solve their own problems.

Effective mentors think systematically about their mentoring practice and learn from experience.

Effective mentors are models of accomplished, self-reliant educators, exemplifying the attributes they seek to inspire in protégés— the capacities that are prerequisites for intellectual growth: the abilities to reason and take multiple perspectives, be creative and take risks, and adopt an experimental and problem-solving orientation.

Effective mentors draw on their knowledge of adult development; subject matter knowledge, curriculum, and pedagogy; and their understanding of their protégés in order to make principled and informed judgments about sound practice. Their decisions are not only grounded in the literature, but also in their experience.

Striving to strengthen their effectiveness, effective mentors critically examine their practice and seek to expand their repertoire; deepen their knowledge; sharpen their judgment; and adapt their field application to new findings, ideas, and theories.

TEACHER MENTOR STANDARDS

Standard I: Context

Effective mentors plan and monitor their behaviors relative to physical and psychological settings that reflect local culture and environment. Mentor activities are appropriately and effectively timed and are aligned with the mission and goals of the school and district. Mentors intentionally act to make their mentoring relationships examples of the kind of norms and positive colleagueship desired in the wider culture of their organization.

Standard II: Content

Effective mentors incorporate into their practice applications designed to meet the assessed professional needs of their protégés. These strategies are based on the principles of adult learning, teacher development, interpersonal communication, coaching, and best practices in mentoring. Wherever possible, mentors use models of effective instruction of students with their protégés, so the protégé experiences the engaging power of effective instruction.

Standard III: Process

Effective mentors gather formal and informal data that describes their protégés' professional performance and how it is evolving based on a model of teacher development that is grounded in research. They apply their knowledge base, application skills, and mentoring expertise based on analysis of those data with the goal of facilitating the protégé's development.

Standard IV: Adjustment

Effective mentors continually seek to add to their knowledge base and application skills. They regularly collect and reflect on data about the protégé's professional growth, the resulting student learning, and their influence on these factors. They modify their practice to ensure that their mentoring is developmentally appropriate for the protégé and to improve protégé and student performance.

Standard V: Collaboration

Effective mentors know that the diverse strengths of a team effort exceed those of any individual. Therefore, they assess their own mentoring strengths and support and promote the involvement of others in their protégés' development, and then they monitor the effectiveness of the array of assistance and facilitate increasing the team's impact. They also help varied communities understand the role of teacher induction and mentoring and—to the extent possible—they involve these communities in the process.

Standard VI: Contribution

Effective mentors seek out and participate in opportunities to advance knowledge and contribute to improving practice among mentoring colleagues and within the field of mentoring.

Source: © 2002 by Hal Portner, Jean Casey, Ann Claunch, and Barry Sweeny. Unpublished.

Resource B

Learning Style Inventory:
Discovering How You Learn Best

Human beings possess five senses—seeing, hearing, feeling, tasting, and smelling. We use these senses to acquire information about the world around us. But we do not all rely on these senses in the same way or to the same degree. This is also true in the acquisition of knowledge. To gain a better understanding of yourself as a learner, you need to evaluate the way you prefer to learn. We all should develop a learning style that will enhance our learning potential. The following evaluation, based on the Barsch Learning Style Inventory, is a short, quick way of assessing your learning style.

Table B.1   Assessing Your Learning Style

Place a check in the appropriate column after each statement.

	Often	*Sometimes*	*Seldom*
1. I can remember more about a subject through listening than reading.			
2. I follow written directions better than oral directions.			
3. I like to write things down or take notes for later review.			
4. I bear down extremely hard with pen or pencil when writing.			
5. I need oral explanations of charts, diagrams, graphs, or other visual materials.			

	Often	*Sometimes*	*Seldom*
6. I enjoy working with tools.			
7. I am skillful with, and enjoy developing or making, charts, graphs, and diagrams.			
8. I can tell if sounds match when presented with a pair of sounds.			
9. I remember best by writing things down several times.			
10. I can easily understand and follow directions on maps.			
11. I do better at academic subjects by listening to lectures and tapes.			
12. I play with coins or keys in my pockets or fidget with objects in my hands.			
13. I learn to spell better by repeating the letters out loud than by writing the word on paper.			
14. I can better understand a news article by reading it in the paper than by listening to the radio.			
15. I like to chew gum, smoke, or snack while studying.			
16. I feel the best way to remember is to picture it in my head.			
17. I learn spelling by tracing or "finger spelling" the words.			
18. I would rather listen to a good lecture or speech than read about the same material in a textbook.			
19. I am good at working and solving jigsaw puzzles, mazes, etc.			
20. I like to grip objects in my hands during study periods.			
21. I prefer to listen to the news on the radio rather than reading about it in the newspaper.			

To determine your learning style preference score, match your responses to the questions above with the corresponding item number below. Place the point value on the line next to the number. Finally, add the points in each column to obtain the preference scores under each heading. For example, if you responded to Question 1 with *Sometimes,* then place a three (3) in the space corresponding to item number 1 in the middle (Auditory) column.

Table B.2   Determining Your Preference Score

Often = 5 points		*Sometimes = 3 points*		*Seldom = 1 point*	
VISUAL		*AUDITORY*		*TACTUAL*	
Item No.	*Points*	*Item No.*	*Points*	*Item No.*	*Points*
2		1		4	
3		5		6	
7		8		9	
10		11		12	
14		13		15	
16		18		17	
20		21		19	
22		24		23	
VPS=		APS=		TPS=	
VPS = Visual preference score		APS = Auditory preference score		TPS: Tactual preference score	

Source: Adapted with permission from the *Learning Style Inventory* developed (1995) by Richard L. Oliver, Ph.D., Student Learning Assistance Center, San Antonio College, San Antonio, Texas.

Resource C

Mentor's Inquiry Process for
Experienced Mentors

The Mentor's Inquiry Process (MIP) is a guide to assist you, an experienced mentor, to enhance and fine-tune your mentoring knowledge, skills, and effectiveness. MIP will help you identify a mentoring-related independent study project and plan the steps you will take to carry it out. Since MIP is a process that allows you to take responsibility for your own learning, you will set your own parameters and time line.

The questions below are intended to stimulate reflection about your mentoring experiences and your thinking about what aspect(s) of your mentoring role you would like to develop further. You might want to write your reflections and thoughts in your journal.

1. What, to you, is the most enjoyable aspect of mentoring? Why?

2. What is the most stressful? Why?

3. Is your mentee motivated by and cooperative in the process? What makes you think so?

4. If you were to describe your major responsibility as a mentor, what would you say?

5. Do you know enough about your mentees and their classroom performance to mentor them effectively?

6. Which of your mentoring abilities is the strongest? Weakest?

7. Do you have a good handle on your mentee's professional needs and what to do to help him/her address them?

8. How do you
   - decide how you will work with your mentee?
   - evaluate the effectiveness of your mentoring?
   - use technology and other resources in the mentoring process?
   - involve other people in your mentoring?
   - incorporate your work as a mentor with other aspects of your work as an educator?

Note: Even though this process can be done independently, you are encouraged to collaborate with your mentoring colleagues in both its planning and implementation stages.

Focus

Reflect on the way things are now in comparison with the way you would like them to be. If there is a difference between these two conditions, *and that difference bothers you,* you probably have identified a significant focus for your project. Write below, in the form of a question, the general focus or topic you would like to pursue. For example: *How might I add structure to the classroom observation process?*

_____

_____

_____

_____

_____

What Will It Be Like?

Imagine that you have successfully solved the problem. Describe that ideal situation. What is happening differently than before? What do you see, hear, smell, taste, feel while carrying it out? What are others saying and doing? What are you saying and doing? Using present tense, write your description below.

_____

_____

_____

_____

_____

ACTIVITIES

Consider the gaps that need to be filled in your abilities, knowledge, skills, and/or understandings in order to address your focus question and to be more specific in how you envision the results of your project. For example: *What kind of observation instruments are there? How can I find out how other mentors structure their classroom observations?*

List several activities you will undertake that will fill those gaps and lead to the realization of your idealized situation. For each activity, estimate start and end dates and list the resource(s) you will consult to accomplish the task. This log will serve as a handy reminder and checklist. You will have the satisfaction of crossing off each activity as it is completed.

_____

_____

_____

_____

_____

What Are Your Chances
of Completing the Activities?

Do you have or can you get what you might need to complete your inquiry in the time you've allowed? Consider the following resources. Will you have enough . . .

- Access to people (who, when, how)?

- Materials (what and who supplies them)?

- Equipment (school's, yours, others)?

- Literature/research (Internet, library, other sources)?

- Time (personal, professional)?

- Personal wherewithal (mental, physical, emotional)?

WHEN DO YOU WANT IT?

What is a realistic date by which you would like to have the inquiry completed?

_____

COSTS

What expenses may be involved? For example:

- Travel _____
- Fees _____
- Materials/equipment _____
- Substitutes _____
- Other _____

DOES IT REPRESENT A WORTHWHILE CHALLENGE?

Can you honestly say that although completing the inquiry will take some effort and stretching, it is achievable and worthwhile?

Yes   No

- Your project should be specific and *observable*.
- It should be realistic and achievable.
- It should be undertaken because you believe that it will add to the value to your mentoring efforts.
- As you carry out your independent study, you may need to add, omit, or alter certain activities or even the project itself. By all means, do so.
- The rest is up to you. The time and energy devoted to this need not be excessive, but it will be effective if well planned and implemented.

Resource D

The Connecticut Competency Instrument

The Connecticut Competency Instrument (CCI) was developed and validated during the late 1980s and early 1990s for the purpose of assessing the teaching competencies of a beginning teacher that are observable in the teacher's classroom.

There are several assumptions embodied in the holistic approach represented by the CCI that are important for mentors of new teachers to understand if they intend to use the instrument to inform their mentoring behaviors. These assumptions are the following:

- Effective teaching can take many forms.
- Critical dimensions of teacher performance that promote learning can be defined across diverse educational contexts.
- The competence of beginning teachers as decision makers can be differentiated from that of experienced teachers.
- Effective teaching is sensitive to cultural diversity.
- Effective teaching must be judged in the context of the teacher's objectives.
- Professional judgment is vital to teacher assessment.

The CCI consists of ten indicators organized into three clusters of competencies that can be thought of holistically as aspects of the instructional process. The clusters are (a) management of the classroom environment, (b) instruction, and (c) assessment of students' understanding. In each of these areas, the focus of the instrument is primarily teacher behavior, but the impact on student behavior in the classroom is also critical.

Following is the text of the CCI, reprinted with permission from the Connecticut State Department of Education.

I. MANAGEMENT OF THE CLASSROOM ENVIRONMENT

IA. The Teacher Promotes a Positive Learning Environment

The teacher is responsible for the nature and quality of teacher-student interactions in her or his classroom. The teacher's perception of students and their abilities directly affects students' responses, motivation, and achievement. The teacher's interactions with students should be positive and designed to enhance the learning environment. The beginning teacher, therefore, establishes and maintains a positive learning environment by creating a physical environment conducive to learning and maintaining both positive teacher-student and student-student interactions.

Defining Attributes

There are three defining attributes of promoting a positive learning environment. They reflect the use of a variety of techniques for promoting positive teacher-student interactions and a physical environment that is conducive to learning:

(1) Rapport: The teacher establishes rapport with all students by demonstrating patience, acceptance, empathy and/or interest in students through positive verbal and non-verbal exchanges. The teacher avoids sarcasm, disparaging remarks, sexist and racial comments, scapegoating and physical abuse. The teacher also exhibits her or his own enthusiasm for the content and for learning and maintains a positive social and emotional atmosphere in the learning environment.

(2) Communication of expectations for academic achievement: The teacher creates a climate that encourages all students to achieve. Expectations for success may be explicitly verbalized or communicated through the teacher's approach to assigning tasks, rewarding student effort and providing help and encouragement to all students.

(3) Physical environment: To the extent it is under her or his control, the teacher establishes a physical environment that is safe and conducive to learning.

IB. The Teacher Maintains Appropriate Standards of Behavior

Research shows that effective teachers use management practices that include concrete, functional and explicit rules and standards that are established early in the school year and maintained throughout the year. Fitting consequences should be applied to both appropriate and inappropriate behaviors. Teachers' standards or rules may vary, but their use in the management of behavior should assist in effectively facilitating the teaching-learning process in the classroom. The beginning teacher will maintain these standards through clear and consistent expectations for appropriate student behavior.

Defining Attribute

There is one defining attribute for the process of maintaining appropriate standards for behavior:

(1) Rules and standards of behavior are maintained: Either through explicit statements of rules or through responses to student behavior, the teacher communicates and reinforces appropriate standards of behavior for the students. The teacher applies fitting consequences when student behavior is either appropriate (i.e., consistent with the standards) or inappropriate. Even though a teacher's standards may vary, they should have the effect of facilitating student learning. A pattern of appropriate behavior indicates that rules and standards have been previously communicated to the students. A pattern of inappropriate behavior indicates that rules and standards of behavior are not being maintained.

IC. The Teacher Engages the Students in the Activities of the Lesson

The amount of time students spend on the tasks of the lesson is important because it is a reflection and outcome of the teacher's management and instructional skills. Research consistently shows that the amount of time students spend successfully engaged in activities relevant to the lesson objectives is positively related to student achievement. Conversely, time spent disengaged or off-task is associated with low achievement gains. This indicator assesses the engagement of students in the activities of the lesson.

Defining Attributes

There are two defining attributes for engagement of students:

(1) Student engagement: The beginning teacher engages a clear majority (at least 80 percent) of the students in the activities of the

lesson. Engagement is defined as students' involvement in lesson activities consistent with the teacher's expectations or directions. Although a high rate of engagement is expected, it is acceptable for students to be momentarily off-task from time to time during a lesson.

(2) Re-engagement: When students are persistently off-task, the teacher must attempt to bring them back on task. A variety of strategies may be used. A teacher's attempt to re-engage a student need not be successful; however, when unsuccessful, the teacher must make additional attempts to re-engage the student.

ID. The Teacher Effectively Manages Routines and Transitions

How teachers allocate and manage the administrative and organizational activities of the classroom has a direct bearing on the amount of time that is available for instruction, and the quality of that instruction. Whereas Indicator IC is concerned with the amount of instructional time in which students are actually engaged in learning activities, Indicator ID deals with how the teacher manages the non-instructional time. It is expected that the beginning teacher will effectively use the time allocated for instruction by managing routines and transitions to support the purposes of instruction.

Classroom routines are non-instructional, organizational, administrative or repetitive activities such as roll-taking, pencil-sharpening or the distribution of materials and equipment, although the latter may be in preparation for subsequent instruction. Transitions are non-instructional organizational or administrative moves from one classroom activity or context to another. Transitions may occur between instructional activities as well as between an instructional and a non-instructional activity.

Defining Attribute

There is one defining attribute of the management of routines and transitions:

(1) Effectiveness: The teacher should provide effective routines and transitions that reflect planning, established norms and a sense of structure. When appropriate, resources and materials should be organized and available. In addition, the amount of time spent on routines and transitions should be appropriate for their purpose and

the makeup of the class. Depending upon the nature and purpose of a routine or transition, proceeding too quickly may be as detrimental as taking too much time with the non-instructional activities.

II. INSTRUCTION

Assessor judgment about the acceptability of teacher performance on the instruction indicators rests heavily on the clarity of the teacher's objectives. Beginning teachers must have clear and specific objectives for their lessons or for all learning activities. (Indicators IIA, IIB, IIC, and IID relate directly to the lesson objective.) It is important, therefore, for beginning teachers to fully understand what the students are expected to learn and clearly convey that understanding to assessors through the Pre-Assessment Information Form and Pre-Observation Interview. The Post-Observation Interview gives teachers an opportunity to indicate any changes made in their objectives or activities during the course of the lesson, or any unexpected classroom occurrences that could impact the observation.

There are frequent references to lesson elements within the indicators of the instruction cluster. These are discrete parts of a lesson, the beginnings or endings of which may be indicated by a change in activity, topic, or instructional arrangement.

IIA. The Teacher Presents Appropriate Lesson Content

Research shows that teaching is most effective when content is both accurate and at a level of difficulty or complexity appropriate for the learners. The competent beginning teacher should demonstrate mastery of the subject matter through the representation and delivery of accurate content. The content of the lesson should also be aligned with the objectives of the lesson. Content includes, but is not limited to, lesson materials, student discussion, activities, practice, modeling, demonstrations, teacher presentation, and teacher questioning.

Defining Attributes

There are three defining attributes for assessing the lesson content:

(1) Choice of content: The content must be aligned with the lesson objectives. Teachers should not significantly deviate from the lesson content as specified in the objectives, unless the objectives or activities are modified during the lesson.

(2) Level of difficulty: The lesson content must be at a level of difficulty (neither too easy nor too hard) that is suitable for the level of students' cognitive development. Content should also be at an appropriate level for the students' social, emotional and/or physical development. The teacher will use vocabulary and language appropriate to the learners. The appropriate level of difficulty may differ among students, and often the appropriateness may be judged by student responses and behavior.

(3) Accuracy: The lesson content must be accurate. Infrequent, minor inaccuracies not significantly related to the content should not be considered in the rating of this defining attribute.

IIB. The Teacher Creates a Structure for Learning

The beginning teacher is responsible for providing the structure in which learning occurs. A consistent research finding is that when teachers appropriately structure instructional information, student achievement is increased. Research shows that initiations facilitate student understanding. Research suggests that closures assist students in integrating and processing information, and practitioners and education specialists believe it is an important part of lesson structure. Lesson elements are discrete parts of a lesson, the beginnings or endings of which may be indicated by a change of activity, topic or instructional arrangement.

Defining Attributes

There are two defining attributes of creating a structure for learning:

(1) Initiations: Initiations must relate to lesson objectives and help students anticipate or focus on the lesson content. The beginning teacher will provide initiations at the beginning of the lesson or between significant instructional elements throughout the lesson. Frequently, initiations preview what is to be learned, why it is to be learned, or how it relates to past or future learning. Initiations have a role in motivating students. Initiations may be explicit statements or may occur through established instructional activities or teacher modeling tied to the lesson objectives. Simply stating the activities in which the students will engage is not sufficient for initiation.

(2) Closures: Closures must relate to lesson objectives and help students understand the purpose of the lesson content. The beginning teacher is responsible for closure at the end of the lesson or between significant instructional elements throughout the lesson. Simply restating lesson objectives is not sufficient for closure.

IIC. The Teacher Develops the Lesson to Promote Achievement of the Lesson Objectives

Development is the heart of the lesson and the key to establishing meaning for students and achieving lesson objectives. It is in developing the lesson that the teacher organizes instructional activities and materials to enhance students' learning of lesson content. Effective development motivates and moves students toward the lesson objectives. In an effectively developed lesson, related elements are manifestly linked to each other, and the materials and instructional arrangements contribute to the lesson's momentum. Lesson elements are discrete parts of a lesson, the beginnings or endings of which may be indicated by a change of activity, topic or instructional arrangement.

Defining Attributes

There are two defining attributes of effective lesson development.

(1) Lesson development: Effective lesson development (a) provides an underlying order within and among lesson elements, (b) manifests a link between related lesson elements, and (c) leads students to learn the content of each element.

Effective lesson development integrates these three components into a conceptual whole that establishes meaning for students and moves them toward achieving the lesson objective(s). The content of the lesson element(s) must be related to the lesson objective(s).

(2) Use of instructional arrangements and materials: Materials and instructional arrangements must purposefully support the development of the lesson. They should be used to promote student interest and involvement in the lesson.

IID. The Teacher Uses Appropriate Questioning Strategies

Questioning is an important aspect of instruction that stimulates and develops students' thinking and helps communicate what is to be learned. Questioning strategies also involve students, encourage the exchange of ideas or information between and among students and assist students in meeting the lesson objectives. Questioning may be explicit and verbal or may be implicitly embedded in lesson materials or activities. When using explicit questioning, the competent beginning teacher waits for and listens to student answers, effectively responds and incorporates those answers into the lesson. Questioning may be explicit and verbal or may be implicitly embedded in lesson materials or activities. Questioning includes any activity the teacher uses to obtain student oral, written or non-verbal responses to the content of the lesson.

Defining Attributes

There are three defining attributes that are applied to assess questioning:

(1) Cognitive level: The level of questioning must be appropriate to the lesson objectives. If the teacher is seeking recall of basic facts or concepts, then questions of a lower cognitive level are appropriate. If the teacher's purpose is to stimulate higher-level thinking, such as analysis and evaluation, then questions of a higher cognitive level are appropriate. In many lessons, a variety of questioning levels will be appropriate.

(2) Responding to students: The teacher should respond to student replies, failures to answer, questions, and/or comments. Where appropriate, the teacher builds upon student contributions to work toward the lesson objectives. Responses may include waiting, clarifying, refocusing, acknowledging correct responses, providing corrective feedback, extending, or prompting.

(3) Opportunities for student involvement: Opportunities for student involvement must be provided by allowing all students an opportunity to answer the question(s) and seeking answers from a variety of students. Opportunities may include student-initiated questions and tasks as well as teacher-initiated questions. Appropriate use of wait time allows all students an opportunity to become involved in questioning activity.

IIE. The Teacher Communicates Clearly, Using Precise Language and Acceptable Oral Expressions

The quality of teacher communication is important for student learning. Teachers should provide clear presentations and explanations of the lesson content. Precise communication and clear speech should serve to enhance student understanding. Teachers are expected to model acceptable oral expressions.

Defining Attributes

There are three attributes that define acceptable teacher communication:

(1) Precision of communication: Precision of communication refers to the communication of meaning. The teacher must communicate in a coherent manner, avoiding vagueness and ambiguity that interfere with student understanding. Precision of communication includes giving directions.

(2) Clarity of speech: Clarity of speech refers to the technical quality of communication. This consists of the teacher's articulation, volume and rate of delivery, which must not interfere with student understanding.

(3) Oral expressions: A pattern of unacceptable oral expressions must be avoided. Incorrect grammar and slang should be avoided; however, it is acceptable for teachers selectively to use current popular phrases or slang to make a point, establish rapport or enhance the learning. Vulgarity should be avoided.

III. Assessment of Student Progress

Assessor judgment about the acceptability of teacher performance on the assessment indicator rests heavily on the clarity of the teacher's objectives. Consequently beginning teachers must have clear and specific objectives for their lessons for all learning activities. It is important, therefore, for beginning teachers to fully understand what the students are expected to learn and to clearly convey that understanding to assessors through the Pre-Assessment Information Form and Pre-Observation Interview. The Post-Observation Interview gives teachers an opportunity to indicate any changes in planned objectives or activities made as a result of monitoring.

IIIA. The Teacher Monitors Student Understanding of the Lesson and Adjusts Instruction When Necessary

The importance of monitoring and adjusting is underscored by research on teaching. More learning will occur when teachers regularly monitor their students' understanding and adjust instruction when appropriate. The two components support one another in promoting student understanding; appropriate adjustment is contingent upon sufficient monitoring and should not be viewed separately. The beginning teacher should monitor students' understanding at appropriate points in the lesson and adjust her or his teaching when the resulting information indicates it is necessary to do so. Lesson elements are discrete parts of a lesson, the beginnings or endings of which may be indicated by a change of activity, topic or instructional arrangement.

Defining Attributes

The Indicator has two defining attributes:

(1) Monitoring for understanding: The purpose of monitoring is to see that students are understanding the lesson content and moving toward the lesson objectives. Toward this end, the teacher must check the level of understanding of a variety of students at appropriate points during the lesson. These points include (but are not limited to) the completion of a lesson element and after an adjustment resulting from monitoring.

(2) Adjusting when necessary: The teacher must use appropriate strategies to adjust his or her teaching when monitoring or spontaneous student response indicates that students are misunderstanding or failing to learn. Strategies for adjustment may include representing information, re-explaining a concept, asking different types of questions, and/or slowing the pace of instruction. The teacher will also use appropriate strategies to adjust when monitoring indicates that students have mastered the concepts being taught. Such strategies may include accelerating the pace of instruction, providing enrichment activities, and/or moving on to new material. When monitoring indicates that adjustment is necessary but not possible within the lesson, the teacher must acknowledge to the students the need for adjustment at a later time.

Source: Reprinted with permission from the Connecticut State Department of Education.

Resource E

Annotated Bibliography

The publications I have chosen to include in this bibliography are selected from among the many books and articles about induction and mentoring written over the last two and a half decades. The selection also includes writings that, although not specifically about mentoring, illustrate and expand upon the research and models that inform the functional behaviors associated with mentoring new teachers.

I have made this an annotated bibliography, rather than simply a list of references, because I want to entice you, the reader, to inquire further into various aspects of mentoring. It provides a comprehensive and panoramic view of what is available should you want to increase your knowledge base and sharpen your mentoring effectiveness.

Bartell, C. A. (2005). *Cultivating high-quality teaching through induction and mentoring.* Thousand Oaks, CA: Corwin Press.

> The material in this book is built around the recognition of the challenges facing beginning teachers in general and the special challenges imposed on new teachers teaching in an urban setting. Bartell draws upon her long-time involvement with the California Beginning Teacher Support and Assessment program to provide both a vision and set of strategies that translate induction policy into practice. In the course of the book, she provides insights into stages of teacher development, identifies characteristics of effective induction programs, and describes examples of best practices in mentoring. Additional chapters focus on standards-based teaching, reflective practices, and standards-driven assessment.

Boreen, J., Johnson, M. K., Niday, D., & Potts, J. (2000). *Mentoring beginning teachers.* York, ME: Stenhouse.

Mentoring Beginning Teachers is organized around the discussion of a series of key questions: Why be part of a mentoring experience? Why do we need mentors? How do I prepare to be a mentoring guide and coach? How do I address classroom management challenges? How do I encourage reflection and professional development?

In the process of answering these questions, the authors provide examples of teachers' journal entries, anecdotes, and reflective writings. They also include recommendations for mentor/ beginning teacher pairings, questions to open collegial conversations, and prompts to encourage teacher reflection. Finally, drawing from their own experiences, a group of mentors respond to questions from novices with practical ideas and suggestions supported by sound theoretical principles.

Boreen, J., & Niday, D. (2003). *Mentoring across boundaries.* York, ME: Stenhouse.

Part I of this book discusses and makes suggestions about some of the typical concerns of mentoring providers, such as choosing and supporting good mentors. It is Part II, however, that adds much less discussed, yet just as critical, dimensions that impact the mentoring process: the school environment and the personal and interpersonal challenges that may arise in the relationship between mentor and mentee. Specific issues the authors explore include age, gender, and culture in the mentoring relationship; new teachers in urban or rural settings; veteran teachers in new schools; working with at-risk students; and using technology to support mentoring.

Breaux, A., & Wong, H. (2003). *New teacher induction: How to train, support, and retain new teachers.* Mountain View, CA: Harry K. Wong Publications.

"First and foremost, we have written this book to share the stories of successful programs with you and provide you with a basic how-to approach—a blueprint for structuring a successful new teacher induction program" (p. vi). This is how Annette L. Breaux, a public school curriculum coordinator, and Harry K. Wong, a highly regarded speaker and educator, describe the purpose of their book. *New Teacher Induction* carries out their stated intention and does so in a colorful and reader-friendly format.

The stories of more than 30 successful programs, including several in countries other than the United States, are described through the book—many in detail, others as vignettes. Photographs, graphs, and forms illustrate and clarify many of the examples. The authors emphasize the importance of a comprehensive, coherent, and sustained induction program and provide details for structuring such a system. The elements of a successful induction program are described, along with a process for its implementation.

A sampling of frequently asked questions and an extensive reference section are included. The references consist of journal articles, examples of induction structures, information materials, and data tables.

Throughout the book, the authors convey their belief that "the inability to attract and retain highly qualified teachers is the most significant problem we face in education today, because without effective teachers, our children cannot receive quality education" (p. vi).

Brewster, C., & Railsback, J. (2001). *Supporting beginning teachers: How administrators, teachers, and policymakers can help new teachers succeed.* Portland, OR: Northwest Regional Educational Laboratory. [Available from http://www.nwrel.org]

The Northwest Regional Educational Laboratory is one of ten research and development regional educational laboratories supported by contracts with the United States Department of Education's Office of Educational Research and Improvement. This booklet is the sixteenth in a series of "hot topic" reports produced by the Northwest Lab to address current educational concerns. *Supporting Beginning Teachers* contains a discussion of research and literature, implications for policy and practice, and a sampling of how Northwest educators are addressing the issue.

Specifically, the booklet contains sections discussing the benefits of providing mentoring support and implementing a formal program. Also discussed are ways individuals can contribute to the program, suggestions for beginning teachers, special considerations for rural schools, supporting bilingual and minority teachers, consideration for policymakers, and teacher union support. Descriptions of mentoring programs in Montana, Washington, and Oregon are included as well.

Brock, B. L., & Grady, M. L. (2007). *From first-year to first-rate: Principals guiding new teachers* (3rd ed.). Thousand Oaks, CA: Corwin Press.

Although this book is written for administrators who want to develop an effective induction plan for first-year teachers, much of the material and discussion applies equally to the role and function of the mentor. The authors look at the diversity of beginning teachers and what those differences imply in terms of induction. They go on to identify problems beginning teachers face and examine the varied social cultures of schools and the difficulties teachers may encounter as they try to adapt their to specific school contexts. Guidelines for helping new teachers and supporting mentors are presented. The authors also outline a plan for integrating induction and career-long development.

Brookfield, S. D. (1995). *Becoming a critically reflective teacher.* San Francisco: Jossey-Bass.

Applying the principles of adult learning, Brookfield tells teachers how they can reframe their teaching by examining their practices from the perspectives of their own experiences as teachers and learners, the perceptions of their students and colleagues, and the lessons of theory. Throughout the book, he describes strategies and practical approaches to critical reflection, including the use of teaching diaries, role model portfolios, participant learning portfolios, structured critical conversation, and the Good Practices Audit—a process in which teachers search their experiences for good responses to common problems they encounter. Brookfield devotes a chapter to negotiating the risks and apparent contradictions of critical reflection and ends his book with an argument for the creation of a culture of reflection.

Carkhuff, R. R. (1993). *The art of helping* (7th ed.). Amherst, MA: Human Resource Development Press.

Robert Carkhuff's helping process begins with what he calls "the most profound step: relating interpersonally" and culminates with "empowering people to actualize their own human potential" (p. i). The seventh edition discusses the helping process in terms of the helpee's and helper's contribution to the process. The author also describes and provides examples of four helping skills—attending, responding, personalizing, and initiating—to which the main body of his book is devoted. A comprehensive list of feeling words appears in the appendix.

Chernyak, L. (2006). *Induction malfunction: Leaving teachers behind.* Bloomington, IN: AuthorHouse.

This comprehensive study showcases what happens to novice teachers, specifically at a Florida charter middle school, when a mentored induction program is purposefully and neglectfully disbanded. The book documents the points of view of three novice teachers who—despite efforts to collaborate, grow professionally together, and take lessons learned from the first year into the next—witness firsthand how easily promises made can be broken, how easily the building of collaborative bridges can be burned, and how hard incorporating highly regarded education theories into practice can be. By recording in detail the yearlong experience of these novice teachers, Chernyak paints a picture of realism about their trials and tribulations in terms of their professional lives and growth in an environment lacking collaborative support.

Claxton, C. S., & Murrell, P. H. (1987). Learning styles: Implications for improving education practices. *ASHE-ERIC Higher Education Report No. 4.* Washington, DC: Association for the Study of Higher Education.

Claxton and Murrell examine various approaches to understanding how people learn and classify these approaches in terms of personality, information processing, social interaction, and instructional methods. The authors then describe models that have been developed in each of the four classifications and discuss their potential applications.

Personality models discussed include Herman A. Witkin's Field Dependence-Independence Dimension of Cognitive Style, which determines the extent to which a person is influenced by the surroundings and the ramifications of that degree of influence; the Myers-Briggs Type Indicator, which considers the ways in which people take in information and how they choose to make decisions; the Reflection Versus Impulsivity model, which contrasts the tendency to reflect over alternative solution possibilities with the tendency to select impulsively; the Omnibus Personality Inventory, which measures long-term intellectual, interpersonal, and social-emotional development; and the Holland Typology of Personality, which posits six personality types: Realistic, Investigative, Social, Conventional, Enterprising, and Artistic.

Information processing models discussed are those by Gordon Pask, who looks at the way people approach learning in terms of holistic versus serialistic strategies; by Siegle and Siegle, who describe a continuum ranging from factual to conceptual learning preferences; by Schmeck, who classifies information processors by devoting more attention to the meaning and classification of an idea suggested by a symbol rather than to the symbol itself; by David Kolb, whose experiential learning model describes learning as a four-step cyclic process incorporating concrete experience, reflective observation, abstract conceptualization, and active experimentation; and by Anthony Gregorc, who postulates that learning occurs both through concrete experience and abstraction, either randomly or sequentially.

Social interaction models were developed by Mann et al., who categorize learners into eight behavioral clusters: compliant, anxious-dependent, discouraged workers, independent, heroes, snipers, attention seekers, and silent; by Grasha and Reichmann, who classify learners as independent, dependent, collaborative, competitive, participant, or avoidant; by Fuhrmann and Jacobs, whose model involves dependent, collaborative, and independent styles; and by Eison, who identifies style in terms of attitude toward grading and learning.

Instructional preference models discussed are by Joseph Hill, who maps and interprets the learning style preferred by the learner, such as symbols, culture, influence, memory, cognition, teaching style, and decision making; and by Albert Canfield, who is concerned with conditions of learning (affiliation, structure, achievement, and eminence) and the content of learning (numerics and logic, language, things, and people).

The authors suggest that by understanding our own and others' learning preferences, we can become, and help others become, more active participants in the learning process.

Colton, A. B., & Sparks-Langer, G. M. (1993). A conceptual framework to guide the development of teacher reflection and decision making. *Journal of Teacher Education, 44*(1), 45–54.

The authors have developed what they term "a conceptual framework that portrays the mental processes [of teachers who are] reflective decision makers" (p. 45). As part of the process of reflective decision making, Colton and Sparks-Langer see teachers considering the immediate and long-term social and ethical implications of their decisions.

The article touches on cognitive psychology, critical theory, and theories of motivation and caring, the background theories upon which the framework is based. It then presents the framework itself, which integrates cognitive, critical, and personal characteristics. The authors identify seven categories of knowledge in a reflective teacher: content, students, pedagogy, context, prior experiences, personal views and values, and scripts. The framework also identifies three categories of action related to decisions: planning, implementation, and evaluation. The authors contend that knowledge and meaning are constructed as teachers interpret reality in light of their professional knowledge base; that feelings have an influence on the ability to reflect; and that efficacy, flexibility, social responsibility, and consciousness supported by a collegial environment drive and support teacher reflection.

Correia, M. P., & McHenry, J. M. (2002). *The mentor's handbook.* Norwood, MA: Christopher-Gordon Publishers.

Although *The Mentor's Handbook* addresses several aspects of mentoring, its major contribution is to the refinement of one of the basic mentoring functions—coaching. It does so through a Cycle of Conferencing organizer that guides the mentor through the process of deciding what to observe during a classroom visit, collecting relevant data during that observation, and using the collected data to improve teaching. Five methods for gathering observation data (Word for Word, Keeping Track of Time, Mapping the Classroom, Measuring Methodology, and The Sights and Sounds of the Classroom) are presented in a clear and logical format. The authors provide examples of the application of these methods and suggestions about how they can be linked to teaching standards and professional development.

Costa, A., & Garmston, R. (2002). *Cognitive coaching* (2nd ed.). Norwood, MA: Christopher-Gordon Publishers.

This truly comprehensive work—probably more than any other—has provided practitioners with the vocabulary, historical perspective, strategies, and ideal of the coaching cycle that forms the backbone of contemporary mentoring. The authors describe cognition and instruction in depth, as well as coaching basics—for which they provide a well-stocked toolbox of techniques. Costa and Garmston discuss the element of trust in the coaching process and offer ways to develop and maintain it. Among the resources provided are twelve principles of constructivism that the authors argue guide cognitive coaches.

Costa, A., Garmston, R., Zimmerman, D., & D'Arcangelo, M. (1988). *Another set of eyes: Conferencing skills, trainer's manual.* Alexandria, VA: Association for Supervision and Curriculum Development.

The authors present and discuss the techniques needed for effective cognitive coaching. Included are the conferencing skills of questioning, listening, paraphrasing, and probing for specificity. Activities that provide opportunities for practice are provided and a supplementary videotape is available.

Crow, G. M., & Matthews, L. J. (1998). *Finding one's way: How mentoring can lead to dynamic leadership.* Thousand Oaks, CA: Corwin Press.

This book was written for school leaders who want to develop and enhance leadership qualities in themselves and others by means of the mentoring process. The authors see mentoring as having three functions: the development of knowledge, skills, behaviors, and values; career satisfaction, awareness, and advancement; and attention to personal and emotional well-being.

The authors discuss such pragmatic concerns as mentor selection and training and provide an overview of mentoring as a career-long process. Although the focus of the book is on the socialization and mentoring of principals and assistant principals, it also is relevant to teachers.

Cullingford, C. (Ed.). (2006). *Mentoring in education: An international perspective.* Burlington, VT: Ashgate.

This book is an academic critique of the concept and application of mentoring in Europe, the United States, and the Middle East. The contributing authors examine empirical studies, including case studies and analysis of current practice, with an eye to comparing differences between the theoretical and everyday realities of mentoring as it is practiced in various countries.

Denmark, V. M., & Podsen, I. (2000). The mettle of a mentor. *Journal of Staff Development, 21*(4), 18–22.

The authors of this article identify and discuss six competencies of an effective mentor: understand the mentor role, initiate the relationship, establish a climate of peer support, model reflective teaching practices, apply and share effective classroom management strategies, and encourage and nurture an appreciation of diversity.

Dilts, R., Grinder, J., Bandler, R., Bandler, L. C., & DeLozier, J. (1980). *Neuro-linguistic programming: Vol. 1., The study of the structure of subjective experience.* Cupertino, CA: Meta.

In the early 1970s, Richard Bandler and John Grinder, by virtue of collecting and analyzing the communication styles and structures of successful psychotherapists, found themselves in possession of what they saw as a set of powerful and effective communication models. This book generalizes these models for use in other areas of human communication—specifically, business, law, and education.

The introduction and several chapters of the book describe in detail the structure and system of Neuro-Linguistic Programming, the mechanics and implications of its strategies, the form and content of its utilization in various settings, and rules of thumb in designing and redesigning its form.

Chapter 3, "Elicitation," and Chapter 4, "Utilization," are the two chapters most applicable to mentoring new teachers. Chapter 3 goes into detail about eye movements as assessing cues to sensory modalities and also describes the assessing cues of gestures, breathing, posture, muscle tone, vocal tone, and tempo of speech. Chapter 4 introduces pacing. Briefly, pacing is the process of feeding back to another person, through your own behavior, the behaviors and strategies that you have observed in them—that is, going into their model of the world and becoming synchronized with their own internal process—thereby building rapport and trust.

Duffy, M. J., & Forgan, J. (2005). *Mentoring new special education teachers.* Thousand Oaks, CA: Corwin Press.

This book focuses on the challenges facing the new special education (SPED) teacher and the specific support a mentor can provide such as collaborating with general educators, making accommodations, individualized education programs, and instructional strategies. Also discussed are issues of identifying and training SPED mentors. Most chapters conclude with Web sites for mentors and what-if questions for mentors to consider.

Dunne, K., & Villani, S. (2007). *Mentoring new teachers through collaborative coaching: Linking teacher and student learning.* San Francisco: WestEd.

The first chapter in this book concentrates on the conceptual shift of mentor-as-buddy to mentor-as-learner. It touches on the steps in developing a mentor program and discusses the elements of an effective program. Chapter 2 is about the mentor's role and responsibility, Chapter 3 puts into perspective the teacher's first year, and the fourth chapter takes the reader through the collaborative coaching cycle. A companion Facilitation and Training Guide provides activities, training agenda, and other resources to guide the designing and implementation of effective mentor professional development.

Fast, J. (1970). *Body language.* New York: M. Evans.

> *Kinesics,* as the author calls the study of body language, is based on the behavioral patterns of nonverbal communication. It can include any nonreflexive or reflexive movement of a part or all of the body, used by a person to communicate an emotional message to the outside world. Using a number of anecdotes and examples, Fast shows how both the delivery and reception of body language can greatly enhance and enrich verbal communication. He also warns that the cultural nuances of body language can lead to misinterpretation.

> Included in Fast's survey of the topic are considerations of such aspects of body language as social and public space; facial expressions; touch; posture; eye contact; the movement and positioning of arms, legs, and hands; and how people—often unconsciously—may contradict as well as support their words with their behavior.

Fletcher, S. (2000). *Mentoring in schools: A handbook of good practice.* London: Kogan Page Ltd., and Herndon, VA: Stylus Publishing.

> The author is a lecturer and researcher at the University of Bath in England; consequently, the section titled "Further Reading" in this book includes many pertinent titles not usually found in reference or resource listings in American publications. The book's 20 chapters are divided into five parts: Developing Your Mentoring, The Process of Mentoring, Mentoring in the School Context, Contexts for Mentoring, and Developing Competence Through Mentoring. Included among these five sections are chapters dealing with, for example, structured mentoring, giving feedback, engaging in reflective practice, planning lessons with your mentee, mentoring within a subject area, and appraising competence. Each chapter ends with a summary of good practice.

Fraser, J. (2000). *Teacher to teacher: A guidebook for effective mentoring.* Westport, CT: Heinemann.

> In *Teacher to Teacher*, Fraser describes and draws upon the experiences and principles that have developed and guided her as a successful mentor. The book suggests ways for a mentor to

establish and nurture a mentoring relationship and help mentees with classroom management. The author also addresses the importance of reflection in the mentoring process; helping the mentee with the application of learning theories, especially active learning, in the classroom; and guiding the mentee on ways to work productively with parents.

Gordon, S., & Maxey, S. (2000). *How to help beginning teachers succeed* (2nd ed.). Alexandria, VA: Association for Supervision and Curriculum Development.

The authors begin by identifying six pervasive difficulties many beginning teachers encounter that are major causes of the high rate of teacher attrition: unclear expectations, inadequate resources, isolation, role conflict, difficult work assignments, and reality shock. They go on to suggest twelve specific needs imbedded in those difficulties and postulate that the way to address those needs is through a beginning teacher assistance program.

Discussed in this book are ways to develop such a program. Chapters deal with the selection of mentors, needs assessments, forms, and summative program evaluation. A listing of selected resources for practitioners is included.

Gottesman, B. (2000). *Peer coaching for educators* (2nd ed.). Lanham, MD: Scarecrow Press.

Peer Coaching for Educators presents in detail a five-step process for what the author describes as "a simple, nonthreatening structure designed for peers to help each other improve instruction or learning situations" (p. 2). The steps, which can also apply to coaching new teachers, are (1) request a visit, (2) visit, (3) review notes and list some possibilities, (4) talk after the visit, and (5) process review.

Also discussed is peer coaching's relationship to teaching portfolios, evaluation and supervision systems; how peer coaching can change school culture; and the roles of the various players involved in a peer coaching program.

Graham, P., Hudson-Ross, S., Adkins, C., McWhorter, P., & Stewart, J. (Eds.). (1999). *Teacher/mentor: A dialogue for collaborative learning* (Practitioner Inquiry Series). New York: Teachers College Press.

Teacher/Mentor chronicles and draws insights from several years of experience by a group of teacher-educators, middle and high school teachers, and preservice teacher candidates working to remodel teacher education. Although its focus is on the teacher/mentor dynamics within the secondary school language arts milieu, much of the material relates to other levels and subject areas. Some of the situations presented in the book describe guidelines, activities, and problem-solving methods used. Other scenarios discuss relationships among mentors and student/beginning teachers. The book is written from the perspective of the teachers involved in the collaboration and provides a realistic taste of their mission and methods, as well as the outcomes of their efforts.

Hartzel, G. N. (1990). Induction of experienced teachers into a new school site. *Journal of Staff Development, 11*(4), 28–31.

This article from the National Staff Development Council's informative journal highlights differences between novice teachers and experienced newcomers and suggests six areas that principals (and I would add mentors) need to address with experienced teachers who are new to the school: (1) a realistic view of the school, (2) the emotional aspects involved in the transition, (3) the informal socialization process, (4) appropriate reallocation of tasks, (5) involvement in important tasks, and (6) the provision of regular feedback.

Hicks, C. D., Glasgow, N. A., & McNary, S. J. (2005). *What successful mentors do.* Thousand Oaks, CA: Corwin Press.

This book is subtitled *81 Research-Based Strategies for New Teacher Induction, Training, and Support.* The authors present each of these strategies using the same format: the strategy itself, what the research says about it, how it can be applied, precautions and possible pitfalls, and reference sources. The strategies are grouped into ten sections or chapters, allowing the reader to readily pick and choose—if so desired—rather than read the book sequentially. The first chapter contains approaches for choosing the best strategies. The others have to do with what mentors need to know about new teachers to help them succeed. Groupings of strategies include supporting new teachers as they interact with students, manage classrooms and curriculum, evaluate students, develop teaching styles, work with special needs and diverse students, use technology, and develop relationships with parents and community.

Hiemstra, R., & Brockett, R. G. (Eds.) (1994). Overcoming resistance to self-direction in adult learning. *New directions for adult and continuing education, 64.* San Francisco: Jossey-Bass.

One of the tasks of a mentor is to help mentees take increasing responsibility for their own learning. The intent of this publication is to help readers understand some of the sources of resistance to self-directed learning and to identify strategies to overcome such resistance. The eleven chapters are written by people who have carried out research related to self-direction in learning in a variety of settings. They explore myths that contribute to resistance; discuss key terms, strategies, and techniques for overcoming resistance; examine the literature related to the topic; propose portfolio assessment as a particular strategy; describe how self-directed learning has been used in continuing education by various professional groups, including physicians and architects, and for career advancement by power utility employees; describe how technology and psychometric instruments have been used to enhance and measure individualized learning; and suggest several aspects of the learning process over which learners can assume some control.

Jonson, K. F. (2002). *Being an effective mentor: How to help beginning teachers succeed.* Thousand Oaks, CA: Corwin Press.

After a discussion of the mentor's qualifications, role, training, and programmatic issues, Jonson asks readers to recall their preservice training and first days of teaching. She provides and illustrates a variety of mentoring strategies, discusses phases of adult learning and of mentoring relationships, and presents some pitfalls and payoffs of being a mentor. Resources include month-by-month mentoring activities, mentor-mentee action plans, a framework of teaching competencies, a first-day checklist, and a supervisory beliefs inventory.

Kolb, D. A. (1984). *Experiential learning.* Englewood Cliffs, NJ: Prentice Hall.

Kolb builds on the concept of experiential learning as it emerged in the works of Dewey, Lewin, and Piaget and analyzes its contemporary applications in education, organization development, management development, and adult development. Of special interest to mentors are Chapters 4—"Individuality in Learning and the Concept of Learning Styles"—and 7—"Learning and Development in Higher Education." Kolb's Learning Style Indicator is described and discussed at length in Chapter 4, and the consequences of matches and mismatches between learning style and teaching styles in Chapter 7.

Lee, G. V., & Barnett, B. G. (1994). Using reflective questioning to promote collaborative dialogue. *Journal of Staff Development, 15*(1), 16–21.

Lee and Barnett contend that reflective questioning—a technique in which one person prepares and asks questions that are designed to provide opportunities for the respondent to explore his or her knowledge, skills, experiences, attitudes, beliefs, and values—is a skill that can be developed and used by educators with peers, clients, supervisors, students, and mentees.

This article, based on the authors' experiences teaching the skill, includes information about the origin of the strategy, describes various forms of reflective questioning, delineates conditions that support its use, and provides guidelines for formulating and asking reflective questions.

Lipton, L., & Wellman, B. (2001). *Mentoring matters: A practical guide to learning focused relationships.* Sherman, CT: MiraVia LLC. (Distributed by Christopher-Gordon Publishers, in Norwood, MA)

In *Mentoring Matters*, Wellman and Lipton emphasize a critical aspect of mentoring that, unfortunately, is often underplayed by other authors: combining mentoring behaviors with contemporary teaching-learning theories. The book's nine sections provide strategies and tools to effectively support that concept. For example, Section I anticipates the month-by-month needs of new teachers and emphasizes the need for balance between support and challenge. Other sections offer a continuum of most-to-least directive stances for mentor-mentee interactions; present structured strategies to guide planning, reflection, and problem solving; provide tools to enhance mentoring skills, create emotional safety, and encourage complex thinking; and suggest ways to support the growth of mentees throughout their developmental stages. The publication contains a rich and varied collection of supportive resources, including rubrics for assessing the mentoring relationship, standards for beginning teachers, and portfolio development ideas.

Manthei, J. (1990). *Mentor-teacher preparation inventory and guide for planning and action.* Boston: The Massachusetts Field Center for Teaching and Learning.

This is a self-assessment instrument for teachers who plan to serve as mentors and is designed to be used before a mentorship begins. The instrument is divided into two sections. The first asks the teacher to summarize personal qualities and professional skills using a Likert-type scale. In the second section, the teacher uses the first section's descriptors to assess mentor preparation needs and plan for acquiring additional skills and knowledge.

Massachusetts Teachers Association & Massachusetts Field Center for Teaching and Learning. (1990). *The first year.* Boston: Author.

In May 1990, the Massachusetts Teachers Association, in collaboration with the Massachusetts Field Center for Teaching and Learning, convened a group of first-year teachers to identify their needs. This is the 23-page report of the results of that process. The report is divided into two sections. The first summarizes the written and oral responses of the new teachers to open-ended questions about their preparation, experiences, successes, and failures. It then makes recommendations and offers advice to new teachers in general. The second section examines where the new teachers learned the skills and acquired the knowledge necessary to teach and how they would redesign the components that went into their preparation. Of special interest to mentors are the new teachers' reactions to their introduction to the school community; their formal orientation; and their relationships with administrators, veteran teachers, school staff, teachers union, and parents.

McEwan, E. K. (2002). *10 traits of highly effective teachers: How to hire, coach, and mentor successful teachers*. Thousand Oaks, CA: Corwin Press.

10 Traits of Highly Effective Teachers is written with the results-oriented administrator and instructional leader in mind, especially those who want to enhance their ability to recognize and nurture effective teachers. The ten traits that the author has identified fall into three distinct categories: personal traits that signify character; teaching traits that get results; and intellectual traits that demonstrate knowledge, curiosity, and awareness. Each trait is described in terms of its critical attributes, research that links the trait to student achievement, and how mentees can be encouraged in their efforts to become effective teachers through application of these traits.

Resources include a set of graphic organizers, a list of the ten traits with their descriptions, a collection of teacher-candidate interview questions incorporating the traits, and a set of reflective exercises for each trait that can be used by individual teachers or study groups.

Mezirow, J., & Associates. (1990). *Fostering critical reflection in adulthood*. San Francisco: Jossey-Bass.

When confronting new learning situations, adults bring their past experiences, prejudices, and assumptions. Because of this, they often have difficulty seeing new alternatives and adapting to change. This publication presents some specific exercises for helping adult learners reexamine deeply ingrained ways of thinking. The methods presented are based on what the authors call critical reflection, which they describe as recognizing the assumptions underlying one's beliefs and behaviors and trying to judge and justify their rationality in relation to the new learning. In addition to discussing traditional ways to stimulate reflection, such as journal writing, the authors present several less familiar processes including metaphor analysis, video analysis, and concept mapping—a schematic device for representing the relationships among sets of concepts.

Newton, A., Bergstrom, K., Brennan, N., Dunne, K., Gilbert, C., Ibarguen, N., Perez-Selles, M., & Thomas, E. (1994). *Mentoring: A resource and training guide for educators.* Andover, MA: The Regional Laboratory for Educational Improvement of the Northeast and Islands.

This comprehensive training guide for mentoring was developed by staff from state education agencies in Maine, Massachusetts, New Hampshire, New York, and Vermont and staff from The Regional Laboratory for Educational Improvement of the Northeast and Islands. Eight school districts piloted the guidebook and provided feedback for its modification.

The publication contains five sections: (1) Understanding Critical Components of a Mentoring Program, (2) Developing a Mentoring Program, (3) Preparing Mentor-Teachers, (4) Statistics and Stories, and (5) The Launch—Teacher Induction as the Crucial Stage of the Professional Development Journey. Each section briefly reviews the research and literature on that topic; suggests additional resources; and includes relevant activities supported by directions, handouts, and masters for overheads. Taken together, the 800-page loose-leaf compendium provides a systematic structure for planning, implementing, and sustaining a mentoring program in the public schools.

Odell, S. J., & Huling, L. (Eds.). (2000). *Quality mentoring for novice teachers.* Bloomington, IN: Kappa Delta Phi.

The National Commission on Professional Support and Development for Novice Teachers was established in 1996 by the Association of Teacher Educators and Kappa Delta Phi International Honor Society in Education with the objective of making recommendations for improving and enhancing the policy, practice, and process of mentoring preservice and novice teachers. This publication summarizes the recommendations made by that commission, contains a summary of current induction programs in the United

States, conceptualizes and furnishes background information on quality mentoring, and provides a mentoring framework to guide the development and assessment of quality mentoring practice.

The mentoring framework is organized into six dimensions: program purposes; school, district, and university cultures and responsibilities; mentor selection and mentor/novice matching; mentor preparation and development; mentor roles and practice; and program administration, implementation, and evaluation. Each dimension is discussed in depth and supplemented by activities to assist universities and school systems in studying the mentoring process.

Olsen, K. D. (1999). *The California mentor/teacher role: Owners' manual*. Kent, WA: Books For Educators.

Based on her extensive work with the California State Department of Education and other educational experiences, the author provides thoughtful discussions about the role of the mentor, what makes a mentor effective, and the mentoring process in general. Descriptions of mentoring concerns such as working with adults in terms of brain-based learning, effective communication styles for adults, and various coaching models are supplemented by the judicious use of graphics and reinforced with reflective exercises. An extensive glossary defines the specialized terms and concepts used throughout the book.

Pelletier, C. (2006). *Mentoring in action*. Boston: Allyn and Bacon.

Subtitled *A Month-by-Month Curriculum for Mentors and Their New Teachers*, this book walks the mentoring pair through a full year of exercises. Each month's activities are structured under sections labeled Plan, Connect, Act, Reflect, and Set Goals. The book's appendix provides a unique set of templates for quality conversations with new teachers in blocks of time ranging from five minutes to two hours.

Pitton, D. E. (2006). *Mentoring novice teachers: Fostering a dialogue process* (2nd ed.). Thousand Oaks, CA: Corwin Press.

Mentoring Novice Teachers uses examples, role play, and especially dialogue to lead the reader through various mentoring skills and behaviors. Much of the book's emphasis is on the development of the mentoring relationship through trust and communication. Other areas discussed include the diverse needs of the mentee, developing a mentoring framework, data gathering techniques, and program evaluation. A variety of forms and sample action plans support the text.

Podsen, I. J., & Denmark, V. (2007). *Coaching and mentoring first year and student teachers* (2nd ed.). Larchmont, NY: Eye on Education.

This book begins with a discussion of current mentoring attitudes and behaviors. The authors devote the major portion to eight "competency training modules" that are structured to present key factors mentors encounter in the coaching process. These modules are (1) Understanding the Coaching and Mentoring Role, (2) Promoting Collaborative Learning, (3) Nurturing the Novice: Active Cogitative Coaching, (4) Developing Your Performance-Coaching Skills, (5) Modeling and Coaching Effective Teaching Standards, (6) Modeling and Coaching Effective Classroom Management Standards, (7) Displaying Sensitivity to Individual Differences Among Learners, and (8) Willingness to Assume a Redefined Professional Role. Each module contains quotes the authors call "knowledge base highlights," references they term "coaching boosters," relevant exercises, and coaching and mentoring activities. The nine appendices include a variety of forms, templates, and checklists that support the book's focus.

Portner, H. (2001). *Training mentors is not enough: Everything else schools and districts need to do*. Thousand Oaks, CA: Corwin Press.

Training Mentors Is Not Enough postulates that a truly viable and effective mentoring program is tailored to the specific culture and beliefs of the local district and its schools; is built upon a broad base of commitment and participation from all stakeholders; is designed, implemented, managed, assessed, and nurtured within a formal structure of collaborative problem solving and decision making; and receives ongoing support and resources including provision for the ongoing professional development of its people.

The author identifies and discusses the key elements necessary to achieve these conditions: achieving commitment; putting commitment to work; working within the larger system; roles and responsibilities; policies, procedures, and particulars; professional development for newly trained mentors; and evaluating a fledgling mentoring program. Activities, strategies, and examples are provided for each element, along with explicit suggestions for customizing, planning, implementing, and managing them.

Portner, H. (2002). *Being mentored: A guide for protégés.* Thousand Oaks, CA: Corwin Press.

The focus of *Being Mentored* is on the understandings, skills, and behaviors needed by the potential teacher, the student teacher, and the new teacher who expect to profit from being a recipient in the mentoring process.

Discussion, activities, anecdotes, and examples center on such issues as how protégés can contribute to the development and maintenance of mentoring relationships; take responsibility and be proactive in the mentoring process; take advantage of invitations to observe others teach; ask for and receive help; identify what it is they need to learn and how to make decisions about their own professional development; seek out and create opportunities to exchange information and support with their peers; learn by trying something new or doing something differently; critically examine the implications of their experiences in order to learn; and contribute to their schools' programs, procedures, and culture.

Also featured is an annotated compendium of publications and Internet sites of special interest to new teachers.

Portner, H. (Ed.). (2005). *Teacher mentoring and induction: The state of the art and beyond.* Thousand Oaks, CA: Corwin Press.

The twelve chapters of this book are grouped into three sections. Part I, Developing and Designing Induction and Mentoring Programs, describes the developmental processes, organizational structures, and philosophical underpinnings that make up exemplary teacher induction programs.

In Chapter 1, Tom Ganser explains that mentoring programs already have a history that can, in some cases, offset the need to reinvent the wheel when creating new programs or enhancing existing ones and emphasizes the exciting opportunities current research and experience presents for developing even more effective induction and mentoring programs.

In Chapter 2, Mark Bower describes the two-year program development process.

In Chapter 3, Harry Wong documents a variety of programs that eschew teacher retention as their primary goal and focus on teacher effectiveness and student learning.

In Chapter 4, Ellen Moir describes the Santa Cruz New Teacher Project (SCNTP) and what replicating SCNTP in several districts throughout the United States has taught us about the essential components of an effective induction program and the role of mentors.

In Chapter 5, Hal Portner contends that a major task for induction and mentoring program developers is to plan for program survival so that it can sustain and expand its vitality and positive impact on teaching and learning. He presents a set of three principles—systems-thinking, collaborative-doing, and committed-leading—that provide a framework that developers can use for creating the conditions needed to do so.

Part II, Mentoring Constructs and Best Practices, focuses on significant and emerging aspects within the larger context of induction and mentoring.

In Chapter 6, Jean Casey and Ann Claunch trace the five stages of mentor development from novice to expert: predisposition, disequilibrium, transition, confidence, and efficacy.

In Chapter 7, James Rowley articulates the qualities of the good mentor. Rowley discusses institutional resistance to mentor-as-coach, stresses the value of the process, asks policymakers to reflect on where their state or school district program is at the present time in terms of their readiness to embrace the practice.

In Chapter 8, Barry Sweeny argues that people who lead and participate in induction and mentoring programs must purposefully redefine the way they and their institutions use professional time. He offers a variety of strategies for finding, making, and funding time for induction and mentoring and provides examples illustrating the application of some of those strategies.

In Chapter 9, Laura Lipton and Bruce Wellman emphasize the power of mentoring relationships to foster improved student learning. They define the three functions of learning-focused relationships—offering support, creating challenge, and facilitating a professional vision—that distinguish them from other types of possible interaction.

Part III, Connecting Induction and Mentoring to Broader Issues, looks beyond individual programs and practices and examines their extended relationships and interactions.

In Chapter 10, Susan Villani maintains that school communities need to nurture leadership in many different ways if schools are to offer the opportunities for students and adults to learn and achieve at new heights. She suggests that induction and mentoring programs have the potential, perhaps more than any other initiative, to both cultivate and provide opportunity for such leadership.

In Chapter 11, Janice Hall contends that state support of local induction and mentoring is essential. She compares the involvement of states between 1998 and 2004, draws conclusions based on that comparison, and suggests ways such support can be strengthened.

In Chapter 12, Ted Britton and Lynn Paine describe the salient features of comprehensive teacher induction programs they have studied extensively in five countries: China (limited to the city of Shanghai), France, Japan, New Zealand, and Switzerland. Britton and Paine suggest that U.S. induction and mentoring programs in general can benefit greatly by taking a critical look at the components that make up those successful programs.

Each chapter ends with an exercise designed to guide readers through reflecting on the possibilities of applying the chapters' material to their own programs. Finally, Dennis Sparks reminds us that strong induction programs are the starting point of a continuum of professional learning that can extend across a teacher's career.

Reinarz, A. G., & White, E. R. (Eds.). (2001). Beyond teaching to mentoring. *New Directions for Teaching and Learning, 85.* San Francisco: Jossey-Bass.

"Mentoring as Metaphor" by Diane Enerson—the first of eleven articles/chapters by authors from academia—sets the tone of this book by advocating mentoring as a way to focus attention on the learner and on the process of learning. Although the volume examines how college and university faculty might mentor their students, much of the writing can be applied equally well to the mentoring of student teachers and beginning K–12 teachers. For example, one contributing pair of authors addresses stereotypes that can affect mentoring relationships and discusses how mentoring can promote understanding of diversity.

Ribas, W. B. (2006). *Inducting and mentoring teachers new to the district.* Westwood, MA: Ribas Publications.

This book is a synthesis of the author's years of practical experience recruiting, hiring, and inducting new teachers; running district orientation programs; and implementing building support teams. Ribas discusses information and details important dates and times that are important to a new teacher's success. He describes and illustrates classroom management plans and expectations, mentor training, and standards-based lesson planning. The mentor's role in helping mentees to work effectively with parents is also included. Other sections deal with observing and conferencing with mentees and planning for recruitment and induction of teachers new to the school or district.

Richin, R., Banyon, R., Stein, R., & Banyon, F. (2003). *Induction: Connecting teacher recruitment to retention.* Thousand Oaks, CA: Corwin Press.

As the subtitle suggests, this book is written for administrators, teachers, and school board members who participate in recruiting, hiring, developing, and retaining new teachers. The authors present the process in a multiyear "blueprint" composed of five interlocking "building blocks." The blueprint for each block focuses on its goals, participants, and objectives.

Block 1 has to do with preparing to recruit and retain; Block 2 with recruiting, interviewing, and selecting new staff; Block 3 with the first-year sequence of orientation, mentoring, professional development, and supervising new teachers; Block 4 with creating lasting connections during Years 2 and 3; and Block 5 with best practices for retaining high-quality professional staff.

Rowley, J. (1999). The good mentor. *Educational Leadership, 56*(8), 20–22.

The author identifies and discusses six basic qualities of the good mentor and suggests implications these qualities have for entry-year program design and mentor training. The six qualities are (1) commitment to the role of mentoring; (2) accepting of the beginning teacher; (3) skilled at providing instructional support; (4) effective in different interpersonal contexts; (5) modeler of a continuous learner; and (6) communicator of hope and optimism.

Rowley, J. (2006). *Becoming a high performance mentor: A guide to reflection and action.* Thousand Oaks, CA: Corwin Press.

In this book, Rowley articulates further the concepts he defined and communicated in earlier publications that focused on the essential characteristics of the good mentor. Among other devices in this publication, he incorporates vignettes, inventories, models, and questions for reflection to describe quality mentoring, mentor/mentee commitment, acceptance and understanding, patterns of communication, cognitive coaching, teacher learning, and inspirational behavior.

Rowley, J., & Hart, P. (2000). *High performance mentoring kit.* Thousand Oaks, CA: Corwin Press.

Produced primarily for use as a mentor training workshop system, this set of multimedia materials also contains a variety of pertinent concepts and practical material of direct interest to the practicing mentor, such as mentoring styles and behaviors and when to use them. The kit contains a comprehensive facilitator's guide; videotapes of discussions, mentoring strategies, and case studies; a CD-ROM with PowerPoint slides; and a participant's notebook.

Rudney, G. L., & Guillaume, A. M. (2003). *Maximum mentoring.* Thousand Oaks, CA: Corwin Press.

> Covering pretty much all bases, this book takes the reader through the steps of specifying roles, rights, and responsibilities of mentors; understanding unique concerns of student and novice teachers; building relationships; collaborating with university supervision; tending to first-week details; articulating a vision of education; observation and feedback; implementing summative evaluation; working with a teacher in trouble; and growing as a professional. Topics are supported by exercises, forms, checklists, and activities.

Saphier, J., Freedman, S., & Aschheim, B. (2007). *Beyond mentoring: Comprehensive induction programs: How to attract, support, and retain new teachers* (2nd ed.). Wellesley, MA: Teachers.

> The authors present a detailed map for planning a comprehensive induction program for beginning teachers in their first three years of practice. The process's seven components take the reader through the design and management of the program; criteria for selecting and matching mentors with mentees; training, supervision, and support of mentors; services for beginning teachers; budget and policy issues; leadership and whole staff support; and program assessment. Strategies for maintaining and sustaining induction programs are presented along with the influence of induction in the development of a professional learning community. Appendices provide a sample plan, program calendar, and surveys; ideas for providing recognition; and a district self-assessment tool.

Scherer, M. (Ed.). (1999). *A better beginning: Supporting and mentoring new teachers.* Alexandria, VA: Association for Supervision and Curriculum Development.

> This anthology of over two dozen pieces by experienced educators—many of them mentors of new teachers—is an outgrowth of the May 1999 theme issue of Educational Leadership, "Supporting New Teachers."
>
> The six sections in *A Better Beginning* examine the needs of new teachers, new teacher induction, mentoring, comprehensive

reforms, communication and instructional competencies, and attention to fellow practitioners.

The issues discussed in the various sections of the anthology include such topics as support programs for novices, the stages that new teachers go through during their first year of teaching, descriptions of a variety of induction models and mentoring programs, and ways to expand a new teacher's repertoire of teaching strategies.

Sweeny, B. (2008). *Leading the teacher induction and mentoring program* (2nd ed.). Thousand Oaks, CA: Corwin Press.

Leading the Teacher Induction and Mentoring Program addresses new teacher induction and mentoring mainly from the viewpoint of those who are responsible for its effectiveness. The book identifies and discusses various mentoring approaches and structures (e.g., formal/informal, individual/team, full-time/part-time), developing programs and activities as well as people, and strategies for supporting and sustaining induction and mentoring programs. Sweeny uses the Concerns-Based Adoption Model as the basis for clarifying not only beginning teachers' needs, but also those of mentors and induction program designers. He details the gradual implementation of induction programs; describes the components of a "High Impact" induction program; examines mentoring roles and characteristics and their implications; and illustrates exemplary mentor training strategies. The author links induction and mentoring to goals for improved teaching practice and increased student achievement. Sample schedules, templates, and forms supplement many of the book's chapters.

Torres-Guzman, M. E., & Goodwin, A. L. (1995). Mentoring bilingual teachers. *Occasional Papers in Bilingual Education, 12.* Washington, DC: The National Clearinghouse for Bilingual Education.

After a brief discussion of mentoring, the paper reviews the history and nature of mentoring bilingual teachers, examining how and why such mentoring differs from mainstream models. It goes on to point out and discuss at length such salient issues as certification match. It examines the impact of content on the mentor-mentee relationship, highlights concerns about the language and culture of instruction, looks closely at the correlation between language and cognitive development, and touches on the issue of transformation and power relationships. Although the paper does not go into mentoring in other content areas, the principles discussed may be generalized to apply to most disciplines.

Turk, R. L. (1999, May). Get on the team: An alternative mentoring model. *Classroom Leadership Online, 2*(8). [Available from http://www.ascd.org/]

This article discusses, describes, and advocates reciprocal, collegial teaming as an alternative mentoring model.

Udelhofen, S., & Larson, K. (2003). *The mentoring year.* Thousand Oaks, CA: Corwin Press.

This book presents a month-by-month litany of activities, strategies, rubrics, checklists, and templates for supporting new teachers during their first year.

Zachary, L. J. (2000). *The mentor's guide: Facilitating effective learning relationships.* San Francisco: Jossey-Bass.

The Mentor's Guide combines discussion and workbook-like elements to take the reader through processes that range from assessing one's readiness to become a mentor to ways to bring a mentoring relationship to a natural conclusion.

Eight chapters provide a framework for this journey. They start with a self-assessment and discussion of learning style and move on to preparing the environment for mentoring; understanding and progressing through the phases of a mentoring relationship; establishing mentoring goals, priorities, and action plans; listing protocols for addressing stumbling blocks; enabling the mentee; coming to closure; and regenerating personal growth through mentoring. An appendix presents a variety of tools and guidelines for those who administer and supervise mentoring programs.

References

Alsop, R. (2006, February 14). Schools, recruiters try to define traits of future students. *The Wall Street Journal*, p. B6.

Bandler, R., & Grindler, J. (1975). *The structure of magic.* Palo Alto, CA: Science and Behavior Books, Inc.

Breaux, A., & Wong, H. (2003). *New teacher induction: How to train, support, and retain new teachers.* Mountain View, CA: Harry K. Wong.

Brewster, C., & Railsback, J. (2001). *Supporting beginning teachers: How administrators, teachers, and policymakers can help new teachers succeed.* Portland, OR: Northwest Regional Educational Laboratory.

Brock, B. L., & Grady, M. L. (2007). *From first year to first rate* (3rd ed.). Thousands Oaks, CA: Corwin Press.

Correia, M. P., & McHenry, J. M. (2002). *The mentor's handbook.* Norwood, MA: Christopher-Gordon Publishers.

Costa, A., Garmston, R., Zimmerman, D., & D'Arcangelo, M. (1988). *Another set of eyes: Conferencing skills, trainer's manual.* Alexandria, VA: Association for Supervision and Curriculum Development.

Dillon, S. (2007, August 27). With turnover high, schools fight for teachers. *The New York Times.* Retrieved on August 27, 2007, from http://www.nytimes.com

Dilts, R., Grinder, J., Bandler, R., Bandler, L. C., & DeLozier, J. (1980). *Neuro-linguistic programming: Vol. 1, The study of the structure of subjective experience.* Cupertino, CA: Meta.

Dunne, K., & Villani, S. (2007). *Mentoring new teachers through collaborative coaching.* San Francisco: WestEd.

Fuller, F. F. (1969). Concerns of teachers: A developmental conceptualization. *American Education Research Journal, 6,* 207–226.

Ganser, T. (1996). Preparing mentors of beginning teachers: An overview for staff developers. *Journal of Staff Development, 17*(4), 8–11.

Hall, J. (2005). Promoting quality programs through state-school relationships. In H. Portner (Ed.), *Teacher mentoring and induction: The state of the art and beyond* (pp. 213–223). Thousand Oaks, CA: Corwin Press.

Hersey, P., & Blanchard, K. (1974). So you want to know your leadership style? *Training and Development Journal, 28*(2), 1–15.

Hudson, P., Skamp, K., & Brooks, L. (2005). Development of an instrument: Mentoring for effective primary science teaching. *Science Education, 89*(4), 657–674.

Moir, E. (2007). *Ask Ellen.* Retrieved June 29, 2007, from http://www.edu topia.org/ask-ellen-june-2007

National Board for Professional Teaching Standards. (1989). *What teachers should know and be able to do: The five core propositions of the National Board.* Retrieved April 5, 2002, from http://www.nbpts.org/ UserFiles/File/what_teachers.pdf

National Center for Education Statistics. (1997). *Teacher professionalization and teacher commitment: A multilevel analysis.* Retrieved September 1, 2007, from http://nces.ed.gov/pubs/97069.pdf

National Commission on Teaching and America's Future. (2007). *High teacher turnover drains school and district resources.* Retrieved August 27, 2007, from http://www.nctaf.org/resources/news/press_releases/CTT.htm

Pelletier, C. (2006). *Mentoring in action.* Boston: Allyn and Bacon.

Portner, H. (2001). *Training mentors is not enough: Everything else schools and districts need to do.* Thousand Oaks, CA: Corwin Press.

Portner, H. (2002). *Being mentored: A guide for protégés.* Thousand Oaks, CA: Corwin Press.

Portner, H. (2005a). Success for new teachers. *American School Board Journal, 192*(10), 30–33.

Portner, H. (Ed.) (2005b). *Teacher mentoring and induction: The state of the art and beyond.* Thousand Oaks, CA: Corwin Press.

Portner, H. (2005c). *Workshops that really work: The ABCs of designing and delivering sensational presentations.* Thousand Oaks, CA: Corwin Press.

Portner, H., Casey, J., Claunch, A., & Sweeny, B. (2006, March). *Teacher Mentor Standards.* Paper presented at the meeting of the International Mentoring Association Conference, Chicago, IL.

Ribas, W. B. (2006). *Inducting and mentoring teachers new to the district.* Westwood, MA: Ribas Publications.

Rowley, J. B. (2000). *High performance mentoring facilitator's guide.* Thousand Oaks, CA: Corwin Press.

Saphier, J., Freedman, S., & Aschheim, B. (2007). *Beyond mentoring: Comprehensive induction programs: How to attract, support, and retain new teachers* (2nd ed.). Wellesley, MA: Teachers.

Senigo, S. (2001). *History of the Olympics (a lesson plan).* Retrieved October 20, 2006, from http://www.lessonplanspage.com:80/printables/ PSSHistoryOfTheOlympicsFullPlan25.htm

Shyu, J. (2007). *Teacher retention (a blog entry)*. Retrieved June 10, 2007, from http://blogs.edweek.org/teachers/new_terrain/2007/07/why_do_teachers_stay_1.html

Sparks, D. (2005). Afterword: The gift that one generation of educators gives the next. In H. Portner (Ed.), *Teacher mentoring and induction: The state of the art and beyond* (pp. 241–244). Thousand Oaks, CA: Corwin Press.

Sweeny, B. (2005). Mentoring. A matter of time and timing. In H. Portner (Ed.), *Teacher mentoring and induction: The state of the art and beyond* (pp. 129–148). Thousand Oaks, CA: Corwin Press.

Sweeny, B. (2007). *Leading the teacher induction and mentoring program* (2nd ed.). Thousand Oaks, CA: Corwin Press.

Wong, H., & Wong., R. (1999). *The first days of school*. Mountain View, CA: Harry K. Wong Publications.